LIVING IN BAHIA

PHOTOS TUCA REINÉS / TEXT MÔNICA LIMA

LIVING IN BAHIA

EDITED BY / HERAUSGEGEBEN VON / SOUS LA DIRECTION DE

ANGELIKA TASCHEN

TASCHEN

HONG KONG KÖLN LONDON LOS ANGELES MADRID PARIS TOKYO

BRAZIL

BOLIVIA

PARAGUAY

ARGENTINA

BAHIA

Recife •

• Praia do Forte

Salvador

Bahia de Todos os Santos

• Serra Grande

Ilhéus

Porto Seguro •

–Trancoso
–Outeiro das Brisas
–Vila do Outeiro
–Curuípe
–Barra do Prateaçu
–Espelho das Maravilhas
–Caraíva

Prado
Cumuruxatiba

Nova Viçosa

Rio de Janeiro •

São Paulo •

Contents / Inhalt / Sommaire

Casa da Península

PRAIA DO FORTE

Rui Córes, a Portuguese architect now settled in Brazil, designed and built this house, and is proud that the owners allowed him the privilege of selecting its location within a broad swath of the Praia do Forte region on the northern coast of Salvador. This made all the difference, since the house could be envisioned from the outset to make the most of the landscape around it. Named Casa da Península, it was built in 1997 with the instructions that it be rustic, tropical and cosy in style, but with a dainty finish. One of the distinctive features of the house, which occupies more than 1,800 square metres, is what the architect refers to as the "chatter" of running water, an encircling pool that creates a cool, calm ambience. The spacious verandas and the openness of the living spaces, which integrate indoor and outdoor areas, are a defining characteristic of the building, as is the roof thatched with Santa Fé straw, which requires special care in harvesting, drying and particularly the thatching process itself.

Der in Brasilien lebende portugiesische Architekt Rui Córes war sehr stolz, als man ihn auch das Grundstück für das Haus auswählen ließ, das er in Praia do Forte, einem Strand nördlich von Salvador, entwarf und baute. Dadurch konnte er das Projekt bereits mit dem Wissen um die Besonderheiten des Grundstücks planen. Das 1997 errichtete Haus mit dem Namen Casa da Península („Haus auf der Halbinsel") sollte tropisch-rustikal, gemütlich und in hochwertiger Qualität gebaut werden. Eine der Besonderheiten des 1.800 Quadratmeter großen Bauwerkes ist das ewige „Murmeln" des Wassers, das in einem das gesamte Haus umgebenden Wasserbecken fließt und überall für eine frische und beruhigende Stimmung sorgt. Die imposanten Terrassen und die Offenheit der Räume, die Innen- und Außenleben miteinander verbinden, sind ebenso kennzeichnend für die gesamte Konstruktion wie das Strohdach im Santa-Fé-Stil, dessen Herstellung besondere Sorgfalt bei der Ernte und Trocknung der Pflanze sowie der Befestigung der Strohbündel erforderte.

Un des motifs de fierté de Rui Córes, architecte portugais installé au Brésil, est le fait que les propriétaires de la maison qu'il a dessinée et construite l'ont laissé choisir son emplacement, au sein d'une vaste zone de la région de Praia do Forte, sur le littoral nord de Salvador. La maison a ainsi pu être conçue en tirant le meilleur parti du paysage qui l'entoure. Baptisée Casa da Península, elle a été construite en 1997 dans un style rustique-tropical accueillant, selon le désir des propriétaires, mais avec une finition de première qualité. Une des singularités de la maison, dont la surface construite fait plus de 1800 mètres carrés, est ce que l'architecte appelle le « murmure » de l'eau courante : un miroir d'eau qui entoure l'habitation et crée une atmosphère à la fois rafraîchissante et apaisante. Les immenses terrasses et la transparence des ambiances, intégrant les espaces intérieurs à l'extérieur, sont une des caractéristiques de la construction, sans oublier le toit recouvert de paille Santa Fé, qui requiert une attention particulière lors de la récolte, du séchage et surtout lors de la pose.

From a distance, the 560-square-metre infinity pool visually merges with the sea. The gazebo is the ideal place to escape from the sun's rays.

Aus der Ferne gesehen verschmelzen der 560 Quadratmeter große Swimmingpool und das Meer im Auge des Betrachters. Der Pavillon bietet Schutz vor der starken Sonne.

De loin, la piscine de 560 mètres carrés sans parois saillantes est en continuité visuelle avec la mer. Le pavillon est l'endroit idéal pour se protéger de l'ardeur du soleil.

10

PREVIOUS DOUBLE PAGE, LEFT ABOVE:
The balustrade on the veranda of the upper storey rooms combines brickwork with sections of wood to create a lattice for better ventilation.

PREVIOUS DOUBLE PAGE, BELOW LEFT AND RIGHT ABOVE:
The swans glide by on the pools of water that surround the house, bringing a cool freshness into the interior.

PREVIOUS DOUBLE PAGE, RIGHT BELOW:
The furniture on the vast veranda on the main frontage of the house is made of natural fibres.

LEFT:
With its extraordinary size, a concrete column-sculpture featuring a eucalyptus wood frame takes centre stage in the living room.

RIGHT ABOVE:
There is a harmonious blend of concrete and wood in the open area on the lower floor.

RIGHT BELOW:
The eucalyptus shafts supporting the roof double as decoration.

VORIGE DOPPELSEITE, LINKS OBEN:
Für die Balkonbrüstung im Obergeschoss wurde aus Mauern und Holz ein Gitterwerk geschaffen, das für ein besseres Raumklima sorgt.

VORIGE DOPPELSEITE, LINKS UNTEN UND RECHTS OBEN:
Die Schwäne mögen das Wasserbecken rund um das Haus, das auch den Innenräumen Kühle verleiht.

VORIGE DOPPELSEITE, RECHTS UNTEN:
Auf der großen Terrasse am Hauseingang stehen Korbsessel.

LINKE SEITE:
Die Betonsäule in der Mitte des monumentalen Wohnzimmers bringt die Konstruktion aus Eukalyptusbalken zur Geltung.

RECHTS OBEN:
Beton und Holz vereinigen sich harmonisch im Eingangsbereich des Erdgeschosses.

RECHTS UNTEN:
Die das Dach tragenden Eukalyptusbalken wirken sehr dekorativ.

DOUBLE PAGE PRÉCÉDENTE, EN HAUT À GAUCHE :
La balustrade de la terrasse qui entoure les chambres à l'étage allie des parties pleines en maçonnerie avec des parties ajourées en bois favorisant la ventilation.

DOUBLE PAGE PRÉCÉDENTE, EN BAS À GAUCHE ET EN HAUT À DROITE :
Les cygnes animent le miroir d'eau qui entoure la maison et rafraîchit l'intérieur.

DOUBLE PAGE PRÉCÉDENTE, EN BAS À DROITE :
La vaste terrasse située sur la façade principale est meublée en vannerie.

PAGE DE GAUCHE :
La colonne-sculpture en béton au centre de l'immense living met en valeur la charpente en bois d'eucalyptus.

À DROITE, EN HAUT :
Le béton et le bois se marient harmonieusement avec le revêtement de sol de la zone de dégagement, au rez-de-chaussée.

À DROITE, EN BAS :
Les poutres en bois d'eucalyptus qui soutiennent le toit jouent aussi un rôle dans la décoration.

15

CASA DA PENÍNSULA / PRAIA DO FORTE

DAVID BASTOS

PRAIA DO FORTE

Architect David Bastos designed and built his own holiday home in Praia do Forte, an old fishing village 60 kilometres to the north of Salvador. The red house was built on two plots 200 metres from the beach. It catches the prevailing winds and so enjoys pleasant breezes. The house is on stilts, which lends it a special charm. It consists of four sections, or "modules", which separate the social areas from the owner's private quarters. The social area includes the gazebo, the setting for festivities and leisurely weekend lunches, which the party-loving host enjoys enormously. The modules are separated by a single-lane swimming pool and joined by a footbridge. The simplicity of the house's design is underscored by its walls, which lack sharp edges (every corner is rounded). The flooring is white concrete, and eucalyptus wood predominates throughout. The decidedly unconventional landscaping favours green throughout the year.

LEFT PAGE:

The bedroom's outside door opens directly on to the swimming pool. There is no glass in the windows and doors; instead there are adjustable blinds that let the breeze into the house.

RIGHT:

The wooden footbridge joins the house's four "modules". The symmetrical side stairs lead down to the swimming pool (left) and the house entrance (right).

LINKE SEITE:

Der Schlafraum besitzt direkten Zugang zum Swimmingpool. Fenster und Türen sind unverglast; die beweglichen Lamellen der Tür- und Fensterläden sorgen für eine gute Luftzirkulation.

RECHTS:

Der Holzsteg verbindet die vier Bereiche des Hauses. Die symmetrischen Seitentreppen führen links zum Swimmingpool, rechts zum Hauseingang.

PAGE DE GAUCHE :

La porte-fenêtre de la chambre à coucher s'ouvre sur la piscine. Les portes et les fenêtres n'ont pas de vitres, mais des persiennes qui laissent entrer la brise dans la maison.

À DROITE :

La passerelle en bois relie les quatre modules de la maison. Les escaliers latéraux, symétriques, donnent accès à la piscine à gauche et à l'entrée de la maison à droite.

17

Sein Sommerhaus in Praia do Forte, einem alten Fischerdorf rund 60 Kilometer nördlich von Salvador, hat der Architekt David Bastos selbst entworfen und gebaut. Das rote Haus wurde auf zwei Parzellen errichtet, die 200 Meter vom Strand entfernt und immer der Meeresbrise ausgesetzt sind, was im Haus zu einer angenehmen Belüftung führt. Die Pfahlbauweise verleiht dem Haus einen ganz besonderen Charme. Der allgemeine Bereich und die Privaträume des Besitzers sind auf vier Module verteilt und solchermaßen getrennt voneinander. Der offene, wie eine Loggia gestaltete Bereich bietet, ganz dem Geschmack des gastfreundlichen Hausherrn entsprechend, ein stimmungsvolles Szenario für Feste und lange Diners an den Wochenenden. Die vier Module sind zwar durch den Swimmingpool voneinander abgegrenzt, jedoch durch einen Steg miteinander verbunden. Die gewollt fließenden Übergänge spiegeln sich auch in den abgerundeten Kanten der nur angedeuteten Raumbegrenzungen wider. Der Boden ist in weißem Beton gehalten, und in der Einrichtung dominiert Eukalyptusholz. Eine unkonventionelle Gartengestaltung rundet das Bild ab.

C'est à Praia do Forte, une ancienne bourgade de pêcheurs située sur le littoral à 60 kilomètres au nord de Salvador, que l'architecte David Bastos a construit sa maison d'été. De couleur rouge, cette maison a été édifiée sur deux parcelles de terrain situées à 200 mètres de la plage et bénéficiant des vents dominants, ce qui apporte une ventilation très agréable. La construction sur pilotis donne un charme spécial à la maison organisée en quatre modules qui délimitent les espaces ouverts à la vie sociale et ceux réservés à l'intimité du maître de maison. C'est dans cette partie ouverte aux invités que se trouve la terrasse, lieu idéal pour les fêtes et les repas prolongés, particulièrement appréciés de cet hôte amateur de réceptions. Les modules sont séparés par la ligne simple de la piscine et reliés par une passerelle. Le dépouillement du style se remarque sur la maison, avec ses murs sans arêtes (les angles sont arrondis), son sol en ciment blanc et la prédominance du bois d'eucalyptus. L'agencement du paysage, en rien conventionnel, valorise la verdure à toutes les hauteurs.

LEFT ABOVE:
The rustic roof in eucalyptus wood, precision-built by Praia do Forte carpenters, contrasts with the straight sophisticated lines of the furniture.

LEFT BELOW:
The baroque painting by contemporary artist Iuri Sarmento is used as a bedstead.

RIGHT ABOVE:
The social area of the houses has round tables, where there is always room for another guest. There are comfortable sofas in the living room.

RIGHT BELOW:
The contrast between modern and rustic permeates the décor throughout the entire house.

FOLLOWING DOUBLE PAGE, LEFT AND RIGHT:
Views from the pergola to the impeccably equipped gourmet kitchen and the lounge, where handmade ceramic pots are displayed on an old chest.

LINKS OBEN:
Die rustikale Zimmerdecke aus Eukalyptusholz, von Schreinern in Praia do Forte angefertigt, kontrastiert mit den geraden und eleganten Linien des Mobiliars.

LINKS UNTEN:
Das barock anmutende Werk des zeitgenössischen bildenden Künstlers Iuri Sarmento schmückt das Kopfende des Bettes.

RECHTE SEITE OBEN:
Im Gästebereich stehen runde Tische, an denen sich immer ein Platz für einen weiteren Gast findet. In der Lounge lädt das gepolsterte Mobiliar zum Ausruhen ein.

RECHTE SEITE UNTEN:
Der Kontrast zwischen rustikaler und moderner Gestaltung bestimmt die gesamte Hauseinrichtung.

FOLGENDE DOPPELSEITE, LINKS UND RECHTS:
Die Pergola erlaubt Einblicke in die voll ausgestattete Gourmetküche und in die Lounge, in der Keramikvasen auf einer alten Truhe stehen.

À GAUCHE, EN HAUT :
Le plafond charpenté en bois d'eucalyptus, fabriqué méticuleusement par des menuisiers de Praia do Forte, contraste avec les lignes droites et sophistiquées du mobilier.

À GAUCHE, EN BAS :
Le tableau baroque de l'artiste plasticien contemporain Iuri Sarmento sert de tête de lit.

PAGE DE DROITE, EN HAUT :
Des tables rondes sont installées dans les parties communes de la maison ouvertes aux nombreux invités et de confortables canapés garnissent le salon.

PAGE DE DROITE, EN BAS :
Le contraste entre moderne et rustique imprègne toute la décoration.

DOUBLE PAGE SUIVANTE, À GAUCHE ET À DROITE :
La pergola vue depuis la cuisine suréquipée et depuis le salon, avec le coffre ancien sur lequel sont posées des poteries artisanales.

DAVID BASTOS / PRAIA DO FORTE

CAETANO VELOSO

SALVADOR

Caetano Veloso is one of the most brilliant and prodigious Brazilian singers and composers alive today. Born in the little town of Santo Amaro da Purificação, in Recôncavo Baiano, he was still a young man when he moved to Rio de Janeiro, but has remained a frequent visitor to Salvador, the city that was his cultural cradle and where he plans to spend the final years of his life. His house there commands dazzling views of Rio Vermelho's turquoise ocean. As the Veloso family was not the first to live in it, they had to make changes when they bought it, in order to adapt it to their lifestyle. To do so, they called on the services of São Paulo architect Marcelo Suzuki, who not only redesigned the house, but was also responsible for much of its minimalist furniture. The three storeys are connected by a wall with little wooden battens which runs from the lowest part to the upper floor and is based on a painting by Dutch painter Piet Mondrian (1872–1944). There, tucked away in a special corner, among other objects that have meaning for the family, is a hat, which was a gift from the celebrated Brazilian composer Tom Jobim.

LEFT PAGE:

The wooden staircase is supported on a concrete base encrusted with shells, pebbles and shards of glass along with other basic materials.

RIGHT:

In a private corner, the panel displaying photographs is intended as a playful piece and features the names of the artist's two sons Moreno and Zeca.

LINKE SEITE:

In die Betonbasis der Holztreppe wurden Muscheln, Kieselsteine, Glasscherben und andere einfache Materialien eingelegt.

RECHTS:

Die Fotowand in einer privaten Ecke enthält auch die Namen der beiden Söhne des Musikers, Moreno und Zeca.

PAGE DE GAUCHE :

L'escalier en bois s'appuie sur une base en ciment incrusté de matériaux simples, tels des coquillages, des galets ou des morceaux de verre.

À DROITE :

Dans un coin, un tableau ludique composé de photos de famille, avec les prénoms des enfants de l'artiste, Moreno et Zeca, disposés en mots croisés.

Caetano Veloso gehört zu den herausragendsten und kreativsten zeitgenössischen Musikern Brasiliens. Geboren wurde er in Santo Amaro da Purificação, einer kleinen Stadt in der Allerheiligenbucht (Baía de Todos os Santos). Als junger Mann zog er nach Rio de Janeiro, doch immer wieder kehrt er nach Salvador zurück, die Stadt, die ihn kulturell prägte, und wo er eines Tages leben möchte. Hier genießt er vor allem auch die atemberaubende Aussicht auf das türkisblaue Meer des Stadtteils Rio Vermelho. Das Haus, das er und seine Familie dort kauften, musste aber zuerst an ihren Lebensstil angepasst werden. Den Auftrag dazu erhielt Marcelo Suzuki, Architekt aus São Paulo, der das Haus nicht nur vollständig überarbeitete, sondern auch für den Hauptteil der minimalistischen Einrichtung verantwortlich ist. Die drei Etagen sind durch eine vom Unter- bis zum Obergeschoss durchgehende Wand mit einem Holzlattenmuster verbunden, das von einem Bild des niederländischen Malers Piet Mondrian (1872–1944) inspiriert wurde. Neben vielen für die Familie bedeutsamen Gegenständen hängt in einer Ecke der Wand ein Hut – ein Geschenk des berühmten brasilianischen Musikers Tom Jobim.

Caetano Veloso est l'un des chanteurs et compositeurs brésiliens actuels les plus prodigieux. Né dans la petite ville de Santo Amaro da Purificação, au cœur de la baie de Salvador de Bahia, il s'est installé à Rio de Janeiro alors qu'il était très jeune, mais n'a jamais cessé de fréquenter Salvador, son berceau culturel, où il avait déjà fait le projet de vivre un jour. Dans cette maison de Rio Vermelho il jouit d'une vue éblouissante sur la mer couleur bleu turquoise. Comme la construction avait déjà été habitée avant son acquisition par la famille Veloso, elle a dû être adaptée au style de vie des nouveaux propriétaires. L'architecte choisi, Marcelo Suzuki de São Paulo, a non seulement redessiné la maison, mais aussi créé la plupart des meubles minimalistes. Les trois niveaux de la résidence sont reliés par un mur sur lequel des planchettes en bois ont été disposées en s'inspirant d'une œuvre du peintre hollandais Piet Mondrian (1872–1944). C'est là que se trouve, parmi d'autres objets significatifs pour la famille, un chapeau offert par le célèbre compositeur brésilien Tom Jobim.

24

LEFT ABOVE:
The small windows from the original layout of the house have been replaced by large patio doors to help integrate the outdoor view with the inside of the house.

LEFT BELOW:
The dining room, with table and chairs designed by Marcelo Suzuki, is where the swimming pool, garden, kitchen and living room come together.

RIGHT:
The wall connecting the three storeys, based on a work by Piet Mondrian, is adorned with objects that are dear to the owners of the house.

LINKS OBEN:
Die ursprünglich kleinen Fenster des Originalhauses wurden durch große Glastüren ersetzt, um den Blick aus dem Hausinneren nach draußen zu ermöglichen.

LINKS UNTEN:
Das Esszimmer, dessen Tisch und Stühle von Marcelo Suzuki entworfen wurden, ist das Bindeglied zwischen Swimmingpool, Garten, Haus und Wohnzimmer.

RECHTE SEITE:
Gegenstände, die den Hausbesitzern am Herzen liegen, befinden sich auf den Holzlatten an der Wand, deren Muster von einem Gemälde Piet Mondrians inspiriert wurde.

À GAUCHE, EN HAUT :
Les petites fenêtres de la maison d'autrefois ont été transformées en larges portes vitrées afin d'ouvrir la vue et d'intégrer l'espace extérieur.

À GAUCHE, EN BAS :
La salle à manger, dont la table et les chaises ont été dessinées par Marcelo Suzuki, est le point de convergence entre la piscine, le jardin, l'office et le séjour.

PAGE DE DROITE :
Le mur qui relie les trois niveaux, conçu d'après une œuvre de Piet Mondrian, comporte de petites tablettes pour exposer les objets préférés du maître de maison.

CAETANO VELOSO / SALVADOR

DAVID BASTOS

SALVADOR

Brazil's largest bay, Baía de Todos os Santos in Salvador, is also one of the most beautiful in the country. It is so called because it was discovered on All Saints' Day (1st November) 1501. The bay is caressed by a coastline that runs from the railroad suburb to the Farol da Barra lighthouse. Along the way, it passes through Vitória, one of Salvador's most prestigious districts and an enclave of magnificent mansions dating from the early 20th century to the 1980s, when they were replaced by luxury flats. One of these buildings houses the apartment of architect David Bastos. It takes up the entire 25th floor and boasts breathtaking views of the bay and Itaparica island. The 275-square-metre apartment is strikingly minimalist in character, housing what David regards as "staple goods": designer furniture, works of art, books and CDs. The original four rooms on the floor have given way to a new layout, which emphasises social spaces, reflecting the owner's love of throwing parties and having friends round for dinner, in *petit comité*.

LEFT PAGE:
The guiding principle behind the design of the apartment was to emphasise space, openness and views of the horizon.

LEFT:
Helmut Newton's limited-edition book is a key feature of the décor.

LINKE SEITE:
Bei der Planung dieser Wohnung wurde besonderer Wert darauf gelegt, den Raum, die Offenheit und die Sicht zum Horizont maximal zu nutzen.

LINKS:
Einem Buch von Helmut Newton in limitierter Auflage wurde ein Sonderplatz gewährt.

PAGE DE GAUCHE :
L'idée maîtresse est d'essayer de valoriser au maximum l'espace, l'ouverture et la vue sur l'horizon.

À GAUCHE :
Le livre d'Helmut Newton, en tirage limité, occupe une place de choix dans la décoration.

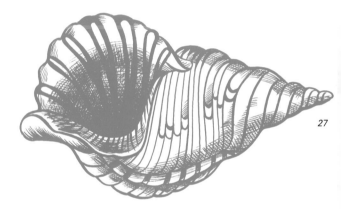

Die größte und auch eine der schönsten Buchten Brasiliens, die Allerheiligenbucht (Baía de Todos os Santos), verdankt ihren Namen ihrer Entdeckung am 1. November 1501. Ihre Uferpromenade säumt die ganze Stadt, dabei geht sie auch am Stadtteil Vitória vorbei, der zu den vornehmsten in Salvador zählt, mit vielen alten, noblen Villen, die allerdings seit den 1980er-Jahren zunehmend von neuen Gebäuden mit Luxusapartments verdrängt werden. In einem solchen Gebäude befindet sich die Wohnung des Architekten David Bastos. Sie umfasst die gesamten 25. Etage und bietet eine atemberaubende Sicht auf die Bucht und auf die Insel Itaparica. Auf den 275 Quadratmetern des minimalistisch eingerichteten Apartments gibt es nur „lebensnotwendige Gegenstände", so Bastos: Designermöbel, Kunstwerke, Bücher und CDs. Die ursprünglichen vier Zimmer sind einem offeneren Raumkonzept gewichen, wo der Hausherr gern Feste veranstaltet oder Freunde im kleinen Kreis zum Essen einlädt.

La Baie de Tous les Saints, la plus étendue du Brésil, est aussi l'une des plus belles du pays. Son nom a pour origine la date de sa découverte en 1501, le 1er novembre, jour de la Toussaint. La baie est sertie d'un rivage qui s'étend du terminal ferroviaire jusqu'au Farol da Barra, en passant par Vitória, l'un des quartiers les plus chics de Salvador. Les belles villas du début du siècle passé ont été remplacées par des immeubles de luxe au cours des années 80. L'appartement de l'architecte David Bastos occupe tout le 25e étage de l'un d'eux, et la vue qui donne sur la baie et sur l'île d'Itaparica est à couper le souffle. Equipé dans un style minimaliste déconcertant, l'appartement de 275 mètres carrés, dans lequel le blanc domine, abrite ce que David Bastos considère comme des « biens de première nécessité » : meubles design, œuvres d'art, livres et CD. Le plan d'origine, avec quatre pièces, a été modifié en un nouvel espace donnant plus de place à la vie sociale. Le propriétaire aime en effet organiser des fêtes et recevoir des amis à déjeuner.

LEFT ABOVE:
The Brazilian-designed wooden chaises-longues have cushions and cotton blankets for comfort.

LEFT BELOW:
The 33-square-metre veranda is an extension of the living room.

RIGHT:
The Saarinen table, surrounded by Philippe Starck chairs, is the perfect place to watch the sun set behind Itaparica island.

LINKS OBEN:
Die Holzliegen in brasilianischem Design sind dank Kissen und Decken aus Baumwolle sehr komfortabel.

LINKS UNTEN:
Die 33 Quadratmeter große Terrasse öffnet und erweitert das Wohnzimmer.

RECHTE SEITE:
Am Saarinen-Tisch mit Philippe-Starck-Stühlen lässt sich der Sonnenuntergang hinter der Insel Itaparica am besten genießen.

À GAUCHE, EN HAUT :
Des coussins et des couvertures en coton apportent un surcroît de confort aux chaises longues en bois de design brésilien.

À GAUCHE, EN BAS :
La terrasse de 33 mètres carrés prolonge le living.

PAGE DE DROITE :
La table Saarinen, avec des chaises Philippe Starck, est le lieu idéal pour assister au coucher du soleil, derrière l'île d'Itaparica.

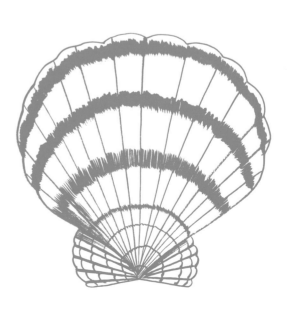

DAVID BASTOS / SALVADOR

LEFT ABOVE:
Of the art books stacked on the shelf, the homeowner's preference is for volumes on design and photography. The sinuousness of the Ray and Charles Eames chair acts as a counterpoint to the straight lines of the sofa by the Italian Antonio Citterio.

LEFT BELOW:
Another combination of a Ray and Charles Eames design, the chairs, paired with an Antonio Citterio design, the table with an opaque glass top.

RIGHT ABOVE:
The concrete floor runs through the whole apartment, linking the spaces and conveying a sense of spaciousness.

RIGHT BELOW:
The kitchen can be joined with the dining room by opening or closing the sliding door.

LINKS OBEN:
Das Bücherregal verrät die Vorliebe des Hausherrn für Design und Fotografie. Die organischen Linien des Eames-Sessels kontrastieren mit dem geradlinigen Citterio-Sofa.

LINKS UNTEN:
Die Stühle sowie der Tisch aus Milchglas bringen wieder die Designer Ray und Charles Eames mit Antonio Citterio kontrastreich zusammen.

RECHE SEITE OBEN:
Der durchgehende Betonboden, mit dem das ganze Apartment ausgestattet wurde, verbindet die Räume und vermittelt den Eindruck von Weite.

RECHTE SEITE UNTEN:
Die Küche kann mithilfe einer Schiebetür dem Essbereich angegliedert oder von ihm getrennt werden.

À GAUCHE, EN HAUT :
Parmi les livres d'art empilés sur l'étagère, la préférence du maître de maison va au design et à la photographie. Les courbes de la chaise de Ray et Charles Eames fournissent un contrepoint aux lignes droites du canapé de l'Italien Antonio Citterio.

À GAUCHE, EN BAS :
De nouveau, l'association du design de Ray et Charles Eames, pour les chaises, et d'Antonio Citterio, pour la table au plateau en verre opaque.

PAGE DE DROITE, EN HAUT :
Dotées du même sol en ciment dans tout l'appartement, les pièces communiquent, ce qui crée une sensation d'espace.

PAGE DE DROITE, EN BAS :
La cuisine peut être intégrée ou non à la salle à manger, grâce à la porte coulissante.

DAVID BASTOS / SALVADOR

HAMILTON PADILHA

SALVADOR

Salvador offers beautiful sunrises over its open Atlantic beaches and sunsets behind Itaparica island, the largest of many in Todos os Santos Bay. The golden evenings, the blue of the sea dotted with little "diamonds" produced by the rays of the sun and the view of the old part of Salvador (where you can make out Bonfim church, one of the city's picture-postcard sights) were the main factors that inspired architect David Bastos to design this flat, which is on a small, quiet street that meets elegant, bustling Corredor da Vitória. The owner, who was born in Salvador but does not live there, wanted the apartment to be simple, spacious, modern and practical, to accommodate him and his friends when they come to stay. With such a stunning view, it wasn't hard to design a space for contemplation. According to the architect, this was one of the reasons he created such a minimalist environment. After all, it would make no sense to hide or compete with the beautiful view.

The afternoon golden light over All Saints Bay (Todos os Santos Bay) is a magical moment. The orange colours bring a feeling of cosiness right into the flat.

Das goldene Nachmittagslicht in der Allerheiligenbucht (Baía de Todos os Santos) ist ein magischer Moment. Die orangefarbenen Töne verleihen dem Apartment eine besondere Atmosphäre.

En fin d'après-midi, la lumière dorée sur la Baie de Tous les Saints est un moment magique. Les tons orangés apportent une sensation de bien-être à l'intérieur de l'appartement.

In Salvador kann man herrlich sowohl die wunderschönsten Sonnenaufgänge über den weiten Atlantikstränden als auch Sonnenuntergänge hinter der Insel Itaparica, der größten der vielen Inseln in der Allerheiligenbucht (Baía de Todos os Santos), beobachten. Das goldene Licht am späten Nachmittag, das in der Sonne wie Diamanten glitzernde Meer und die Sicht auf Salvadors Altstadt mit der bildschönen Bonfim-Kirche waren für den Architekten David Bastos ausschlaggebend, die Gestaltung dieser Wohnung zu übernehmen, die in einer kleinen, ruhigen Querstraße des lauten, eleganten Corredor da Vitória liegt. Auf Wunsch des Besitzers, der in Salvador geboren wurde, aber nicht in der Stadt lebt, sollte das Ambiente schlicht, geräumig, modern und praktisch gestaltet werden, um immer für ihn oder den Besuch von Freunden bereit zu sein. Mit so einer beeindruckenden Aussicht war es nicht schwer, einen kontemplativen Wohnraum zu entwerfen. Sie war auch der Grund für die minimalistische Ausgestaltung des Interieurs, so der Architekt. Schließlich wäre es anmaßend gewesen, die Schönheit der Sicht zu verbauen oder mit ihr zu wetteifern.

Salvador bénéficie à la fois du lever du soleil sur les plages de l'Atlantique et du coucher de soleil derrière l'île d'Itaparica, la plus grande des nombreuses îles de la Baie de Tous les Saints. La lumière, dorée à la tombée du jour, le bleu de la mer parsemé d'éclats de diamants produits par le scintillement du soleil, et la vue sur la partie ancienne de Salvador, où l'on peut apercevoir la célèbre église Nosso Senhor do Bonfim, ont été les principaux points d'appui de l'architecte David Bastos pour réaliser cet appartement situé dans une petite rue calme qui traverse l'élégant et animé Corredor da Vitória. Le propriétaire souhaitait créer une ambiance claire, spacieuse, contemporaine et pratique, car, bien qu'étant né à Salvador, il n'habite pas cet appartement qui lui sert de pied-à-terre ainsi que pour accueillir ses amis. Avec une vue aussi impressionnante, il n'a pas été difficile de concevoir le projet comme un espace de contemplation. C'est d'ailleurs ce qui a donné l'idée de créer une atmosphère minimaliste, selon l'architecte. En définitive, il aurait été injuste de vouloir détourner le regard ou de rivaliser avec la beauté de la vue.

LEFT ABOVE:
The TV room is next to the door to the veranda and is an integral part of the rest of the reception area, which is open-plan. The chaises-longues entice visitors to relax.

LEFT BELOW:
The master bedroom suite makes the most of the beautiful view, with the bed being raised above floor level. A sculpture by Argentinian-Bahian artist Carybé is displayed near the window.

RIGHT ABOVE:
The highlight of the spacious living room, with its cool floor, is the acrylic bar designed by architect David Bastos. The low cabinet runs the whole length of the room.

RIGHT BELOW:
The owner has a valuable collection of art that includes photographs by Mario Cravo Neto and a sculpture by Emanuel Araújo, both Bahian artists.

LINKS OBEN:
Das Fernsehzimmer liegt neben der Terrassentür und ist wichtiger Bestandteil des Wohnbereiches. Die Chaiselongues laden zum Entspannen ein.

LINKS UNTEN:
Um auch im Schlafzimmer die Aussicht genießen zu können, wurde das Bett hochgelegt. Auf der Fensterbank steht eine Skulptur des argentinisch-bahianischen Künstlers Carybé.

RECHTE SEITE OBEN:
Im Wohnzimmer mit kühlendem Steinboden ist die Bar aus Acrylglas ein Blickfang. Von David Bastos entworfen, nimmt sie die ganze Seitenwand des Raumes ein.

RECHTE SEITE UNTEN:
Der Hausherr sammelt in der Wohnung Werke von Künstlern aus Bahia, wie die Fotografien von Mario Cravo Neto oder die Skulptur von Emanuel Araújo.

À GAUCHE, EN HAUT :
La salle de télévision, située à côté de la terrasse, est intégrée à l'espace prévu pour la vie sociale, entièrement ouvert. Les chaises longues invitent à la relaxation.

À GAUCHE, EN BAS :
La suite principale, avec le lit surélevé, permet de profiter d'une vue splendide. Sur le meuble bas, une sculpture de l'artiste plasticien argentin Carybé, qui vit dans l'Etat de Bahia.

PAGE DE DROITE, EN HAUT :
Dans le grand living au sol « froid », le regard est attiré par le bar en plexiglas dessiné par l'architecte David Bastos. Le meuble bas s'étend sur tout le côté de la pièce.

PAGE DE DROITE, EN BAS :
Le propriétaire de l'appartement possède une collection importante d'œuvres d'art, parmi lesquelles des photographies de Mario Cravo Neto et une sculpture d'Emanuel Araújo, des artistes de l'Etat de Bahia.

34

HAMILTON PADILHA / SALVADOR

Casa de Bambu

ANGELINA & ANTONIO BORGES
SERRA GRANDE

Angelina and Antonio Borges live in the coastal paradise of Angra dos Reis, south of Rio de Janeiro, but they have a second home, 100 metres above sea level in Serra Grande, in the Itacaré region. Casa de Bambu was an experimental project conceived by Colombian architect Simón Vélez in close collaboration with the owners. It was built in 2004 using the ranch's own bamboo. The ranch, which covers 160 hectares, lies inside an environmental conservation area, the purpose of which is to preserve the Atlantic Forest. Its overarching goal is to promote the idea of an ecological home, since bamboo is a perennial, renewable resource. An unusual feature is the concrete grass-covered roof to provide thermal insulation and soundproofing. The 200-square-metre house has concrete foundations but rests on bamboo pillars. What in principle was meant to be the prototype of a boutique hotel ended up as a cosy bungalow with two bedroom suites, an American-style kitchen/dining room and a veranda. The family like to treat themselves to long spells there several times a year.

Seen from a distance, the house blends in with its natural surroundings, with its sky blue walls and its grass-covered concrete roof.

Von Weitem scheint das Haus mit den himmelblauen Wänden und dem grasbedeckten Dach mit der Natur zu verschmelzen.

Vue de loin, la maison est totalement intégrée à la nature, avec ses murs bleu azur et son toit en béton recouvert de gazon.

Angelina und Antonio Borges, die in Angra dos Reis leben, einem paradiesischem Küstenort südlich von Rio de Janeiro, besitzen in Serra Grande, in der Region von Itacaré, ein zweites Haus, das dort rund 100 Meter über dem Meeresspiegel steht. Die Casa de Bambu („Bambushaus") ist ein experimentelles Projekt des Architekten Simón Vélez in enger Zusammenarbeit mit den Besitzern. Das Haus wurde 2004 aus Bambus vom eigenen Grundstück errichtet. Zu der Fazenda gehören 160 Hektar Land, das mitten in einem Naturschutzgebiet des Atlantischen Regenwaldes liegt. Oberstes Ziel war es, ein ökologisches Wohnkonzept zu verwirklichen, da Bambus ein erneuerbarer und langlebiger Rohstoff ist. Ein weiteres interessantes Detail ist das mit Gras gedeckte Betondach, was der Wärme- und Schalldämmung dient. Das 200 Quadratmeter große Haus steht auf einem Fundament aus Beton, das aber von Bambussäulen getragen wird. Was ursprünglich als Prototyp für Hotelbungalows gedacht war, ist heute ein gemütliches Wohnhaus mit zwei Schlafzimmern, Wohnzimmer mit integrierter Küche und Terrasse, in dem die Familie mehrmals jährlich lange Aufenthalte genießt.

Habitant Angra dos Reis, sur le littoral sud de l'Etat de Rio de Janeiro, Angelina et Antonio Borges ont une autre maison à Serra Grande, dans la région d'Itacaré, à 100 mètres au-dessus de la mer. La Casa de Bambu est un projet expérimental réalisé par l'architecte colombien Simón Vélez, en étroite collaboration avec les propriétaires. La demeure, qui date de 2004, a été construite avec du bambou provenant directement de la propriété de 160 hectares, située à l'intérieur d'une zone de protection environnementale dont l'objectif est de préserver la forêt atlantique. Le défi majeur de cette maison a consisté à développer le concept d'habitat écologique en utilisant le bambou, un matériau renouvelable et durable. Un autre détail particulier est le toit en béton recouvert de gazon, à la fois isolant thermique et acoustique. La maison de 200 mètres carrés a des fondations en béton mais elle est soutenue par des pilotis en bambou. Ce qui ressemble à première vue à un prototype d'hôtel boutique se révèle être un bungalow accueillant doté de deux suites, d'une salle à manger avec cuisine américaine et d'une terrasse, où la famille aime faire de longs séjours pendant l'année.

LEFT ABOVE:
Even the veranda furniture was designed and made with bamboo.

LEFT BELOW:
The dining-room furniture also has ecological significance: it was made from the dark wood of the pupunha palm. The floor is entirely bamboo.

RIGHT:
The construction of the roof lends it an artistic dimension, thanks to the pattern made by the bamboo rods.

LINKS OBEN:
Auch die Terrassenmöbel wurden aus Bambus gefertigt.

LINKS UNTEN:
Die Wohnzimmermöbel aus dem dunklen Holz der Pfirsichpalme sind ebenfalls ökologisch. Der Boden ist vollständig aus Bambus gefertigt.

RECHTE SEITE:
Die Dachkonstruktion wirkt durch das Muster der Bambusstäbe wie ein Kunstwerk.

À GAUCHE, EN HAUT :
Même les meubles de la terrasse ont été réalisés en bambou.

À GAUCHE, EN BAS :
Le mobilier de la salle à manger respecte aussi l'environnement : il a été fabriqué en bois foncé de pupunha, un palmier indigène. Le sol est en bambou.

PAGE DE DROITE :
La géométrie des tiges de bambou utilisées pour réaliser la charpente du toit apporte une touche artistique.

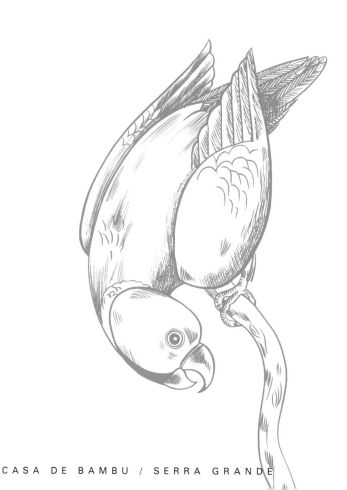

CASA DE BAMBU / SERRA GRANDE

RICARDO SALEM

TRANCOSO

Ricardo Salem was born in São Paulo, grew up in Rio de Janeiro, travelled the world many times over and eventually arrived in Trancoso, an idyllic village on the south coastline of Bahia, in the mid-1970s. At that time, the area was almost unknown, lacking the glamour and vitality it has today. Yet it had something far more precious: the lushness of nature. And thanks to the commitment of people like Ricardo himself, the beautiful landscape remains un-spoiled. The house was the first modern building to be erected in the famous "Quadrado". The Quadrado is a rectangular town square lined with houses and hundred-year-old trees, with a small church at the end nearest the sea. There followed a series of fur-ther houses built by Ricardo, who found there was a demand for his services. The house is just to one side of the church of St John the Baptist, built in 1586 and one of the oldest churches in Brazil. Its construction is based on glass and Atlantic Forest wood, so that the house seems to be an extension of the grove around it.

LEFT PAGE:
*The house has a taubilha
roof, made from wooden
pieces that fit together.*

RIGHT:
*The house is painted in
lime-based paints containing
pigment taken from the soil,
so the colours are all earthy,
ranging from ochre to red.*

LINKE SEITE:
*Das Hausdach besteht aus
miteinander verzahnten
Holzschindeln, die taubilha
genannt werden.*

RECHTS:
*Die Farben, mit denen das
Haus gestrichen ist, basieren
auf einer Mischung aus Kalk
und natürlichen Pigmenten.
Die erdigen Farbtöne reichen
von Ocker bis Rot.*

PAGE DE GAUCHE :
*Le toit de la maison est
couvert de* taubilha *(petites
tuiles en bois).*

À DROITE :
*La peinture utilisée à l'inté-
rieur est à base de chaux
avec des pigments de terre,
ce qui donne ces tons
particuliers variant de l'ocre
au rouge.*

41

Ricardo Salem, geboren in São Paulo, aufgewachsen in Rio de Janeiro und Weltenbummler aus Leidenschaft, kam in den 1970er-Jahren nach Trancoso, einem idyllischen Dorf an der Südküste Bahias. Die Region war damals praktisch unbekannt, fern vom Glamour und von der Dynamik, die sie heute prägen; doch sie hatte etwas viel Kostbareres zu bieten: Natur im Überfluss. Die herrliche Landschaft ist bis heute erhalten geblieben, dank dem Engagement von Menschen wie Ricardo. Sein Haus war das erste moderne Bauprojekt am berühmten Quadrado („Quadrat"), einem großen, rechteckigen Platz, umgeben von historischen Bauten und jahrhundertealten Bäumen und mit einer kleinen Kirche an der zum Meer gewandten Seite. Zugleich war es auch das erste einer Reihe von Häusern, die Salem, heute ein gefragter Bauherr, dort errichtete. Das Haus steht in direkter Nachbarschaft zur Kirche São João Batista, die 1586 gebaut wurde und zu den ältesten Kirchen Brasiliens zählt. Die Baumaterialien des Hauses, Holzarten des Atlantischen Regenwaldes und Glas, holen den Wald in den Wohnraum.

Ricardo Salem est né à São Paulo et a grandi à Rio de Janeiro. C'est après avoir beaucoup voyagé autour du monde qu'il est arrivé au milieu des années 70 à Trancoso, un hameau bucolique du littoral sud de l'Etat de Bahia. La région, alors pratiquement inconnue, loin du prestige et de l'animation actuels, possédait toutefois quelque chose de bien plus précieux : l'exubérance de la nature. Et c'est grâce à l'engagement de personnes comme Ricardo Salem lui-même que ce paysage superbe reste actuellement préservé. Cette maison, la première construction moderne élevée sur le Quadrado, célèbre place entourée de maisons et d'arbres centenaires, sur laquelle se trouve une petite église donnant sur la mer, est également la première d'une série de maisons construites par Ricardo Salem, désormais très demandé. La construction est située juste à côté de l'église São João Batista, l'une des plus anciennes du Brésil, construite en 1586. Les matériaux principaux de la maison sont le bois du littoral atlantique et le verre qui laisse pénétrer la végétation alentour.

LEFT ABOVE:
The swimming pool loungers, chairs and tables were all designed by Ricardo Salem and hand-made in Trancoso.

LEFT BELOW:
The *taubilha* pergola leads into the guest suite, which is in a different module, outside the house.

RIGHT ABOVE:
The old mortar on the earthenware flagstone veranda was sourced from a ranch in the region. The cylinder alongside it, made from vines, is a lamp.

RIGHT BELOW:
The swimming pool, with its sinuous shape, nestles in the lush forest surrounding the house.

LINKE SEITE OBEN:
Die Liegen, Stühle und Tische am Swimmingpool wurden von Ricardo Salem entworfen und von Handwerkern in Trancoso gefertigt.

LINKE SEITE UNTEN:
Die Pergola mit Holzschindeln führt zu den Gästezimmern, die sich in einem vom Haupthaus abgesonderten Bereich befinden.

RECHTS OBEN:
Der alte Stößel auf der mit Tonfliesen ausgelegten Veranda wurde auf einer nahen Fazenda entdeckt. Der aus Lianen gefertigte Zylinder daneben ist eine Stehlampe.

RECHTS UNTEN:
Der Swimmingpool mit seinen geschwungenen Formen ist umgeben vom üppigen Wald, der um das Haus herum wächst.

PAGE DE GAUCHE, EN HAUT :
Les chaises longues, les tables et les chaises autour de la piscine ont été dessinées par Ricardo Salem et fabriquées de manière artisanale à Trancoso.

PAGE DE GAUCHE, EN BAS :
La pergola couverte de bardeaux mène aux appartements des invités, situés dans un module séparé de l'habitation principale.

À DROITE, EN HAUT :
La terrasse en carreaux de brique avec un vieux pilon récupéré dans une ferme de la région. Le billot de cipo, à côté, est un luminaire.

À DROITE, EN BAS :
La piscine, de forme sinueuse, est située au cœur de la végétation luxuriante qui entoure la maison.

RICARDO SALEM / TRANCOSO

LEFT PAGE:
The painting in the living room, by São Paulo artist Franco Cirri (also a resident of Trancoso), is a playful take on the famous Quadrado.

RIGHT PAGE:
The kitchen, where friends get together to enjoy intimate lunches, is one of the most frequented parts of the house and leads directly into the main room.

LINKE SEITE:
Das panneau im Wohnzimmer, eine verspielte Darstellung des Quadrado, ist ein Gemälde von Franco Cirri, einem Maler aus São Paulo, der ebenfalls in Trancoso lebt.

RECHTE SEITE:
Die Küche, in der sich oft Freunde zum Essen treffen, ist einer der meistbenutzten Räume des Hauses und an das Wohnzimmer angegliedert.

PAGE DE GAUCHE :
Dans le living, la peinture sur panneau de l'artiste plasticien Franco Cirri représente de manière ludique la fameuse « place carrée » de Trancoso : le Quadrado.

44

PAGE DE DROITE :
La cuisine, où les amis se réunissent pour les repas, est l'un des espaces les plus fréquentés de la maison. Elle est entièrement intégrée au living.

LEFT ABOVE:
In the living room, which opens onto the forest, pergola and swimming pool, there are miniature canoes, typical of the region and inherited from the indigenous culture.

LEFT BELOW:
The owner's bedroom verges on the monastic: a mattress on the floor, a chaise-longue and a bookcase packed with books meet all his needs.

RIGHT:
The spiral staircase made of sapucaia wood, from Sul da Bahia, connects the three levels of the house: the ground floor, mezzanine and upper floor.

LINKS OBEN:
Im Wohnzimmer, das Zugang zum Wald, zur Pergola und zum Swimmingpool bietet, stehen Miniaturen indianischer Kanus.

LINKS UNTEN:
Das Schlafzimmer des Hausherrn ist fast schon asketisch: Eine Matratze auf dem Boden, ein Liegestuhl und ein Buchregal sind alles, was er braucht.

RECHTE SEITE:
Die Wendeltreppe aus sapucaia, einer Holzart aus Bahia, verbindet die drei Wohnebenen: Erdgeschoss, Mezzanin und Obergeschoss.

À GAUCHE, EN HAUT :
Le living, ouvert sur la végétation, la terrasse et la piscine, est décoré de modèles réduits d'embarcations typiques de la région, héritées de la culture indigène.

À GAUCHE, EN BAS :
La chambre à coucher du maître de maison est quasiment monacale : un matelas à même le sol, une chaise longue et une étagère remplie de livres lui suffisent.

PAGE DE DROITE :
L'escalier hélicoïdal en bois de sapucaia relie les trois niveaux de la maison : le rez-de-chaussée, la mezzanine et l'étage supérieur.

RICARDO SALEM / TRANCOSO

48

Casa do Jacaré

FERNANDO DROGHETTI

TRANCOSO

"Nobody could sleep in the hammock for the house had no walls...". This line from the song by Brazilian poet and composer Vinicius de Moraes fits Casa do Jacaré, the second residence to appear in Trancoso beach, like a glove. Designed by São Paulo architect Sig Bergamin and built by its owner in 1995, it was inspired by the old houses in the region, which dispense with walls, doors and windows for better indoor ventilation. The two modules, which occupy 300 square metres, are built so that only the rooms have walls. And, as with the old houses of inland Brazil, glass is similarly dispensed with. The doors and windows are just hardwood, recycled from a late 19th-century Sul da Bahia ranch. The surrounding landscape is dazzling, since the house occupies a stretch of land between the sea, the Trancoso river and a mangrove swamp, which marks the transition between sea and land and is typical of tropical regions where river and sea converge.

51

„... Niemand konnte in Hängematten schlafen, denn das Haus hatte keine Wände ...", sang einst der brasilianische Musiker Vinicius de Moraes. Sein Text ist wie zugeschnitten auf das Casa do Jacaré („Brillenkaiman-Haus"), das zweite Wohnhaus am Strand von Trancoso. Entworfen wurde es von Sig Bergamin, einem Architekten aus São Paulo, und gebaut von seinem jetzigen Besitzer im Jahr 1995. Als Vorbild dienten alte Häuser der Region ohne Wände, Türen und Fenster zugunsten einer besseren Luftzirkulation im Hausinneren. In den beiden Hausbereichen mit einer Wohnfläche von 300 Quadratmetern haben lediglich die Schlafzimmer Wände. Ebenfalls in Nachahmung einer alten Bauweise aus dem Landesinneren Brasiliens wurde auf Glas verzichtet. Türen und Fenster bestehen aus Massivholz, das von einer alten Fazenda in Südbahia stammt. Das Haus liegt in einer prachtvollen Landschaft, denn das vom Meer, dem Fluss Trancoso sowie von der Mangrovenküste eingerahmte Grundstück bildet eine Passage zwischen Land und Meer, eine typische Landschaftsform in Tropenregionen, in denen ein Fluss auf den Ozean trifft.

« ... On ne pouvait pas dormir dans un hamac, car la maison n'avait pas de murs... » Ce passage d'une chanson écrite par le poète et compositeur Vinicius de Moraes va comme un gant à la Casa do Jacaré, la deuxième maison récemment édifiée sur la plage de Trancoso. Dessinée par l'architecte Sig Bergamin de São Paulo et bâtie par son propriétaire en 1995, elle s'inspire des maisons traditionnelles de la région, ouvertes au maximum pour favoriser la ventilation. Dans cette construction en deux modules d'une surface totale de 300 mètres carrés, seules les chambres à coucher ont des murs. Et, de même que dans les vieilles maisons de l'intérieur du Brésil, il n'y a pas de vitres. Les portes et les fenêtres, en simple bois de construction, proviennent d'une ferme du XIXᵉ siècle du sud de l'Etat de Bahia. Le paysage alentour est éblouissant car la maison est située sur une bande de terre entre la mer, le fleuve Trancoso et une zone marécageuse, typique des embouchures de fleuves des régions tropicales.

LEFT ABOVE:
The wooden taubilha roof, typical of houses in the region, has an opening for the tree trunk to pass through.

LEFT BELOW:
Lush vegetation thrives in the fertile soil. The pipe for the outdoor shower was made from the bark of a piqui tree.

RIGHT:
The straw-covered wooden pergola is where family and friends congregate for meals. The lamp is a converted handmade clay pot.

LINKS OBEN:
Das Dach aus Holzschindeln, typisch für die Region, hat einen Durchlass für den Baumstamm.

LINKS UNTEN:
Grünes wächst rasch und kräftig auf dem fruchtbaren Boden. Die Gartendusche ist aus der Rinde des piqui-Baumes gemacht.

RECHTE SEITE:
Unter der strohgedeckten Holzpergola treffen sich Familie und Freunde zu gemeinsamen Mahlzeiten. Die Lampe ist ein umfunktioniertes Tongefäß.

À GAUCHE, EN HAUT :
Une ouverture a été pratiquée dans le toit de bardeaux, caractéristique des maisons de la région, pour faire place à l'arbre.

À GAUCHE, EN BAS :
La verdure prospère avec vigueur sur ce terrain fertile. La conduite d'eau de la douche a été réalisée avec de l'écorce de piqui, un arbre présent dans cette région.

PAGE DE DROITE :
La pergola en bois recouverte de paille est le lieu où la famille et les amis se réunissent pour les repas. La lampe suspendue a été réalisée à partir d'une cruche artisanale en terre.

CASA DO JACARÉ / TRANCOSO

LEFT:
The living room features authentic Brazilian elements, such as the folding bandeirantes period chair, from the 18th century, the clay pot from northeast Brazil and the collection of gourds hanging from the ceiling.

RIGHT ABOVE:
The table and bench came from the inland region of the state of Minas Gerais. The parquet floor reuses floorboards from demolished old houses.

RIGHT BELOW:
The owner enjoys cooking for his friends, so he joined the kitchen with the living room: he can keep an eye on the saucepans while still taking part in conversations.

LINKE SEITE:
Im Wohnzimmer häufen sich brasilianische Objekte: ein Klappstuhl aus dem 18. Jahrhundert, ein Tongefäß aus dem Nordosten des Landes und eine Kalebassensammlung an der Decke.

RECHTS OBEN:
Tisch und Bänke stammen aus dem Bundesstaat Minas Gerais. Die Dielen des Bodens sind aus altem Abrissholz gefertigt.

RECHTS UNTEN:
Auf Wunsch des Hausherrn, der gerne einlädt, wurde die Küche zum Wohnbereich hin geöffnet, um gleichzeitig kochen und sich unterhalten zu können.

PAGE DE GAUCHE :
Des objets typiquement brésiliens décorent le living : une chaise scoute pliante du XVIIIᵉ siècle, un pot de terre du nord-est du Brésil et une collection de calebasses accrochées au plafond.

À DROITE, EN HAUT :
La chaise et les bancs viennent de l'intérieur du Minas Gerais. Le plancher a été réalisé à partir de matériaux de récupération d'anciennes maisons démolies.

À DROITE, EN BAS :
Le maître de maison aime cuisiner pour ses amis. La cuisine a été intégrée à la salle à manger, ce qui lui permet de surveiller la cuisson tout en participant à la conversation.

CASA DO JACARÉ / TRANCOSO

LEFT ABOVE:
The three-legged stool in this decidedly Brazilian-looking nook was bought at a market. The yellow arch was recycled from a Sul da Bahia ranch.

LEFT BELOW:
The old beds in the girls' bedroom are made of jacarandá wood, nowadays extinct.

RIGHT:
The double bed was made from wood rescued from demolitions and re-covered with local straw. A devotee of St Anthony, Fernando honours him by placing his image in a wall niche.

LINKS OBEN:
Der blaue Hocker vom Straßenmarkt ergänzt die brasilianischen Farben dieses Bereichs. Der gelbe Türrahmen stammt aus einer Fazenda im Süden Bahias.

LINKS UNTEN:
Die antiken Betten im Kinderzimmer bestehen aus Jakarandaholz, einer heute seltenen Holzart.

RECHTE SEITE:
Das Ehebett wurde aus Abrissholz gefertigt und mit Stroh verkleidet. In der Wandnische steht eine Statue des Heiligen Antonius, den Fernando verehrt.

À GAUCHE, EN HAUT :
Dans l'office, le tabouret à trois pieds a été trouvé aux puces. Le cadre de porte jaune provient d'une ferme du sud de l'Etat de Bahia.

À GAUCHE, EN BAS :
Dans la chambre des filles, les lits anciens sont en bois de jacaranda, une essence actuellement en voie de disparition.

PAGE DE DROITE :
Le lit des parents a été fabriqué avec du bois de récupération, revêtu ensuite de paille. Fernando Droghetti a placé une statuette de saint Antoine dans une niche, pour lui rendre hommage.

CASA DO JACARÉ / TRANCOSO

Casa 21

TRANCOSO

The number 21, where possible in orange, has a special meaning for the married couple who own the house. Both are entrepreneurs, living in São Paulo but with their own private paradise at Praia dos Coqueiros, in Trancoso. The property covers 40,000 square metres and the built area covers no fewer than 3,000 square metres, split among seven bungalows. The project was conceived by architect Paulo Jacobsen, who took his cue from the area's natural landscape with its beautiful 100-year-old cashew trees, typical of the northeast of the country. The main bungalow houses the reception areas and, on the upper floor, the 300-square-metre master bedroom suite, which includes the bedroom, two bathrooms and a study. The ground floor houses the living rooms and verandas. Five more bungalows accommodate the couple's seven children and the family's constant flow of guests. Each bungalow is self-contained with two bedroom suites, a living room and kitchen, again on two storeys. The seventh bungalow is a comfortably appointed beach house near the beach and swimming pool.

59

Die Zahl 21 – möglichst orangefarben – hat eine besondere Bedeutung für die Hausbesitzer, ein Unternehmerehepaar aus São Paulo, das in Praia dos Coqueiros, Trancoso, sein eigenes Paradies besitzt. Von dem 40.000 Quadratmeter großen Grundstück sind 3.000 Quadratmeter bebaut und verteilen sich auf sieben Bungalows. Der verantwortliche Architekt Paulo Jacobsen bezog bei diesem Projekt die natürliche umliegende Landschaft ein, die sich durch herrliche jahrhundertealte Cashew-Bäume auszeichnet, eine für den Nordosten Brasiliens typische Baumart. Der Hauptbungalow enthält den Wohnbereich und im Obergeschoss die 300 Quadratmeter große Suite des Ehepaares, die ein Schlafzimmer, zwei Badezimmer und ein Büro umfasst. Das Parterre beherbergt die Wohnzimmer und Terrassen. Fünf der übrigen Bungalows stehen für die sieben Kinder des Ehepaares und für Gäste bereit. Ausgestattet mit je zwei Schlafzimmern, Wohnzimmer und Küche auf zwei Etagen sind sie völlig voneinander unabhängige Einheiten. Der siebte, komfortabel ausgestattete Bungalow am Swimmingpool und Strand dient als Strandhaus.

Le nombre 21 (de couleur orange si possible) possède une signification spéciale pour ce couple d'entrepreneurs de São Paulo, qui a choisi de créer son coin de paradis sur la plage de Praia dos Coqueiros, à Trancoso. La propriété s'étend sur quatre hectares, avec une surface bâtie de 3000 mètres carrés englobant sept bungalows. Le projet est signé de l'architecte Paulo Jacobsen, qui a mis à profit le paysage naturel, où l'on peut voir de superbes anacardiers centenaires, typiques du littoral nord-est brésilien. Dans le bungalow principal, l'espace conçu pour la vie sociale est situé au premier niveau et, à l'étage supérieur, la suite du couple occupe 300 mètres carrés avec une chambre à coucher, deux salles de bains et un bureau. Les livings et les terrasses sont au rez-de-chaussée. Cinq bungalows sont utilisés pour héberger les sept enfants du couple ainsi que les fréquents invités de la famille. Ils sont indépendants et possèdent chacun deux suites, un living et une cuisine, répartis sur deux niveaux. Le septième bungalow est en bord de mer, desservant à la fois la plage et la piscine, avec tout le confort que ces amateurs de réception aiment offrir à leurs invités.

62

PREVIOUS DOUBLE PAGE:
Stopping by to chat by the curving swimming pool is de rigueur after a day on the beach. The natural landscape includes native coconut palms and fruit trees.

LEFT ABOVE:
The swimming pool deck is made of weathered wood, capable of withstanding sun and rain.

LEFT BELOW AND RIGHT:
Nature is present even in the decorative objects: the tree-trunk bench, the natural fibre spheres and the dendê straw ceiling.

VORIGE DOPPELSEITE:
Der geschwungene, von einheimischen Kokospalmen und Obstbäumen umgebene Swimmingpool lädt zum Plauderstündchen auf dem Rückweg vom Strand ein.

LINKS OBEN:
Das imprägnierte Holz um den Swimmingpool hält Sonne und Regen stand.

LINKS UNTEN UND RECHTE SEITE:
Die Natur ist auch in der Einrichtung gegenwärtig: in der Baumstammbank, den Naturfaserkugeln und der Deckenverkleidung aus dendê-Stroh.

DOUBLE PAGE PRÉCÉDENTE :
La piscine au contour ondoyant entourée de cocotiers indigènes et d'arbres fruitiers est une étape obligée pour les discussions au retour de la plage.

À GAUCHE, EN HAUT :
Le sol entourant la piscine est en bois vieilli, résistant à l'action du soleil et de la pluie.

À GAUCHE, EN BAS, ET PAGE DE DROITE :
La nature est présente partout, y compris dans la décoration : le banc réalisé dans un tronc, les sphères tressées en fibre naturelle et le plafond en paille de palmier à huile.

LEFT:
The table is made from the trunk of a tree recovered from the forest around the house. Natural light filters through the straw ceiling during the day and artificial light at night.

RIGHT ABOVE:
The straw pouffes lined up in rows under one of the main bungalow's verandas are like an art installation.

RIGHT BELOW:
The starkly cold minimalism of the sofas, characterised by straight lines, counterbalances the warmth of the table sculpted from a charred tree-trunk.

LINKE SEITE:
Der Tisch ist aus einem Baumstamm gefertigt, der aus dem umliegenden Wald stammt. Tagsüber lässt das Strohdach natürliches Licht in den Wohnbereich einfallen, nachts wird er künstlich beleuchtet.

RECHTS OBEN:
Die gerade aufgereihten Strohpuffs auf einer der Terrassen des Hauptbungalows wirken wie ein Kunstwerk.

RECHTS UNTEN:
Der kühle Minimalismus der geradlinigen Sofas kontrastiert mit der Behaglichkeit des aus einem verkohlten Baumstamm gefertigten Tisches.

PAGE DE GAUCHE :
La table est faite d'un tronc d'arbre récupéré dans la forêt à proximité de la maison. Le plafond en paille laisse passer la lumière du jour ou l'éclairage artificiel la nuit.

À DROITE, EN HAUT :
Sur une des terrasses du bungalow principal, les poufs en paille tressée alignés font figure d'installation artistique.

À DROITE, EN BAS :
Le minimalisme froid des canapés aux lignes droites contraste avec la chaleur de la table-sculpture réalisée dans un tronc d'arbre calciné.

CASA 21 / TRANCOSO

LEFT ABOVE:
The stairs lead up to the master bedroom suite, which has a wooden sliding door.

LEFT BELOW:
The couple's bedroom exudes sophistication and simplicity at the same time. The two straw totems on either side of the bed are actually lamps.

RIGHT:
The room that opens into the veranda, which was originally the dining room, was repurposed as a home for a collection of blue spherical foam pouffes.

LINKS OBEN:
Die Treppe führt zur Hauptschlafzimmersuite, die man durch eine hölzerne Schiebetür betritt.

LINKS UNTEN:
Das Schlafzimmer strahlt Raffinesse und zugleich Schlichtheit aus. Die beidseitig des Bettes aufgestellten Totems aus Stroh sind Stehlampen.

RECHTE SEITE:
Einem ursprünglich als Esszimmer gedachten Raum neben der Terrasse wurde durch die Sammlung von blau umhüllten Schaumstoffpuffs neuer Sinn verliehen.

À GAUCHE, EN HAUT :
L'escalier mène à la suite principale, fermée par une porte coulissante en bois.

À GAUCHE, EN BAS :
La chambre du couple est à la fois simple et sophistiquée. Les totems en paille placés de chaque côté du lit sont des luminaires.

PAGE DE DROITE :
L'espace ouvert sur la terrasse, prévu à l'origine comme salle à manger, a finalement trouvé une fonction différente, avec une collection de poufs sphériques bleus en mousse.

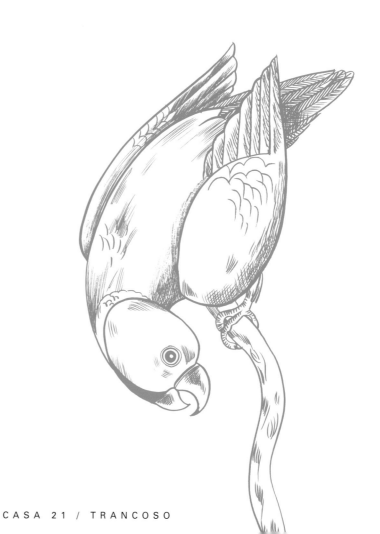

CASA 21 / TRANCOSO

CASA DO GRILO

TRANCOSO

Located next to the mangrove swamp and the beach, Casa do Grilo belongs to one of the many Europeans who fell in love with the colours of the Sul da Bahia landscape: the clear blue of the ocean, the lush green of the vegetation and the golden glow of the sun on the sandy beaches. Under the guidance of architect Sig Bergamin, the house was built with the intention of getting the most from the surrounding nature. Doors and windows were eschewed in order to allow the greenery in. Built from wood and lined with sapé (a natural fibre used as a covering in indigenous houses and colonial properties in inland Brazil), the house occupies an extremely privileged position. Charged with the interior design as well, the architect used organic shades such as khaki, beige and sand, as well as materials such as wood and natural fibres, striving for the utmost integration with nature. The result is a harmonious blend of colours that conveys both sobriety and cosiness.

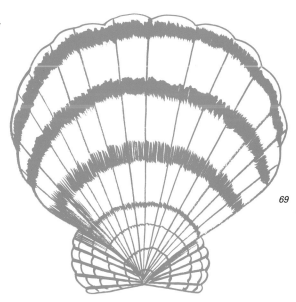

69

Die Casa do Grilo, die zwischen einem Mangrovenwald und dem Strand liegt, gehört einem der vielen Europäer, die sich in die Farbpalette der Landschaft im Süden Bahias verliebt haben: das klare Blau des Meeres, das üppige Grün der Vegetation und den goldenen Glanz des Sandes in der Sonne. Das Haus wurde unter der Anleitung von Sig Bergamin und mit der Absicht errichtet, die umliegende Natur weitgehend einzubeziehen. Auf Türen und Fenster wurde verzichtet, um das Grün bis ins Hausinnere wirken zu lassen. Das Haus, das aus Holz gebaut und mit *sapé* – einer für indianische Bauten und Siedlerhäuser im Landesinneren Brasiliens charakteristischen Naturfaser – gedeckt ist, liegt an einer besonders privilegierten Stelle der Landschaft. Um Haus und Natur zu vereinen, verwendete der auch für die Inneneinrichtung zuständige Architekt vor allem Farben wie Khaki, Beige und Sandtöne sowie natürliche Materialien wie Holz und Naturfasern. Das Ergebnis ist eine Farbharmonie, die sowohl Schlichtheit als auch Wohnlichkeit vermittelt.

Située à proximité d'une zone marécageuse et de la plage, la Casa do Grilo appartient à l'un des nombreux Européens fascinés par les couleurs qui composent le paysage du sud de l'Etat de Bahia : le bleu limpide de la mer, le vert luxuriant de la végétation et l'éclat doré du soleil sur les plages de sable. La maison a été édifiée sous l'égide de l'architecte Sig Bergamin avec l'idée de valoriser au maximum la nature environnante. C'est pourquoi les fenêtres et les portes ont été abolies, afin de laisser entrer l'ambiance de la végétation à l'intérieur de la maison. Avec sa structure en bois et son toit de paille typique des cabanes indigènes et des fermes du centre du Brésil, la maison est disposée de manière stratégique et privilégiée. Egalement en charge de la décoration intérieure, l'architecte a utilisé des couleurs organiques en abondance, comme le kaki, le beige et le sable, ainsi que des matériaux tels que le bois et les fibres naturelles afin d'obtenir une intégration optimale à la nature. Il en résulte une harmonie de couleurs qui évoque la sobriété tout en éveillant un sentiment de bien-être.

LEFT ABOVE:
An outdoor shower under the coconut palms is de rigueur after a swim in the sea.

LEFT BELOW:
The house with its sapé covering is reminiscent of an enormous oca, the name given to the houses of the indigenous population.

RIGHT:
The beachscape changes with the winds and the tide. One benefit of a house by the sea is the continual breeze.

LINKS OBEN:
Eine Dusche unter Kokospalmen ist ein Muss auf dem Rückweg vom Strand.

LINKS UNTEN:
Das mit sapé-Fasern gedeckte Haus erinnert an indianische Bauten, sogenannte oca.

RECHTE SEITE:
Der Anblick des Meeres wandelt sich ständig unter dem Einfluss von Wind und Gezeiten. Eine stete Brise macht das Wohnen direkt am Meer angenehm.

À GAUCHE, EN HAUT :
La douche à l'air libre, sous les cocotiers, est un passage obligé au retour d'un bain de mer.

À GAUCHE, EN BAS :
La maison, avec son toit de paille, évoque une énorme oca, nom donné aux maisons des indigènes du Brésil.

PAGE DE DROITE :
Le paysage de la plage change selon les vents et les marées. La brise constante est un des privilèges des maisons en bord de mer.

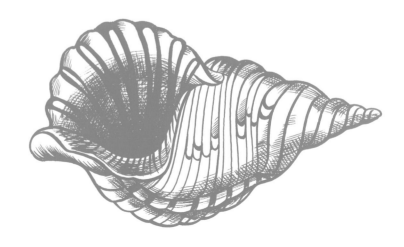

CASA DO GRILO / TRANCOSO

LEFT:
Indigenous wood predominates from top to bottom in the spacious, totally open lounge, which dispenses with doors and windows.

RIGHT ABOVE:
From the upper floor of the oca you can view the long wooden deck surrounded by greenery on all sides.

RIGHT BELOW:
The gazebo is the place of choice for conversation at the end of a long, hot summer's afternoon.

FOLLOWING DOUBLE PAGE:
Symmetry is a trademark of Sig Bergamin, who claims it is necessary in order to achieve equilibrium among the mix of elements he likes to incorporate in the spaces he designs.

LINKE SEITE:
Einheimische Hölzer dominieren rundum. Bei der großen, allseitig offenen Lounge wurde auf Fenster und Türen verzichtet.

RECHTS OBEN:
Vom Obergeschoss des Hauses aus hat man einen Blick auf das hölzerne, vom Grün umgebene Deck.

RECHTS UNTEN:
An heißen Sommernachmittagen ist die Loggia ein perfekter Ort für ein Plauderstündchen.

FOLGENDE DOPPELSEITE:
Ein Markenzeichen von Sig Bergamin ist die symmetrische Anordnung von Raumelementen, mit der er unterschiedliche Gegenstände in ein ausgewogenes Gleichgewicht zu bringen sucht.

PAGE DE GAUCHE :
Les bois indigènes prédominent de bas en haut dans le vaste salon ouvert sur l'extérieur, où portes et fenêtres ont été bannies.

À DROITE, EN HAUT :
L'étage supérieur de la maison offre une vue sur le long pont en bois entouré de verdure.

À DROITE, EN BAS :
La terrasse est l'endroit rêvé pour les conversations estivales de fin d'après-midi.

DOUBLE PAGE SUIVANTE :
La symétrie est une marque de fabrique de Sig Bergamin, qui affirme en avoir besoin pour équilibrer le mélange des éléments qu'il aime composer au sein des espaces qu'il conçoit.

CASA DO GRILO / TRANCOSO

LEFT ABOVE AND RIGHT:
One of the ends of the dining table, made from a section of a tree trunk, extends beyond the bounds of the room and invades the kitchen.

LEFT BELOW:
Half-walls are used in many places as subtle demarcations between spaces. Once again, symmetry is evident in the tables bearing identical objects on both sides.

LINKS OBEN
UND RECHTE SEITE:
Der aus einem Baumstamm geschnittene Esstisch, durchbricht auf einer Seite die Raumgrenze und dringt in die Küche ein.

LINKS UNTEN:
Halbwände deuten hier wie überall im Haus Raumtrennungen an. Die Tische und Gegenstände davor sind wieder symmetrisch angeordnet.

À GAUCHE, EN HAUT, ET PAGE DE DROITE :
Une extrémité de la table servant aux repas, dont le plateau a été découpé dans un tronc d'arbre, dépasse de la salle à manger pour se prolonger dans la cuisine.

À GAUCHE, EN BAS :
Les demi-cloisons ont beaucoup été utilisées pour créer une séparation subtile entre les différents espaces. Une fois de plus, l'effet de symétrie est marquant, avec les tables et les objets identiques des deux côtés.

CASA DO GRILO / TRANCOSO

CASA SAN MARCO

TRANCOSO

Casa San Marco belongs to a family that lives in Paris but has strong ties with Brazil. Three or four times a year, during extended holiday periods, it is not unusual to find the seaside house occupied by fugitives from the European weather enjoying sun, sea and close companionship, gathering for one of their favourite pastimes and watching films in the cinema in the upper floor. The house was built in 2005 to a design by Fabrizio Ceccarelli, an architect originally from Italy and creator of many other houses in the region. At the request of the owners, it was made of wood and glass and built large enough to fit both the family and their friends. Starting from that premise, it was designed so that every room is the same size, which makes life easier for the lady of the house. Another interesting feature is the shape of the terrace, which makes it possible for meals to be eaten in a different place each day.

Die Casa San Marco gehört einer mit Brasilien eng verbundenen Familie aus Paris. Drei- bis viermal im Jahr, meist an verlängerten Wochenenden, belebt sich das Haus, wenn die Besitzer vor dem kalten Klima in Europa flüchten und auf der Suche nach Sonne, Meer und innigem Familienleben nach Bahia kommen. Eine der Lieblingsunternehmungen der Familie hier sind gemeinsame Filmabende im Hauskino im Obergeschoss. Das Haus wurde 2005 von dem ursprünglich aus Italien stammenden Architekten Fabrizio Ceccarelli gebaut, der bereits viele Gebäude in der Region entworfen hat. Den Wünschen der Hausherren entsprechend ist es ganz aus Holz und Glas gemacht und geräumig genug, um nicht nur die Familie, sondern auch Freunde unterzubringen. Letzteres war auch bestimmend bei der Gestaltung der Zimmer, die alle die gleiche Größe haben, was laut Hausherrin vieles erleichtert. Bemerkenswert ist ebenfalls die Form der Terrasse, die es ermöglicht, die Mahlzeiten jeden Tag an einem anderen Platz einzunehmen.

La Casa San Marco appartient à une famille vivant à Paris mais très liée affectivement au Brésil. Trois ou quatre fois par an, ses membres viennent passer les vacances dans cette maison au bord de la mer, fuyant la froideur du climat européen pour profiter du soleil, de la mer et des moments conviviaux, tels que des projections de films dans la salle de cinéma située à l'étage. La maison, conçue par l'architecte d'origine italienne Fabrizio Ceccarelli, auteur de nombreux projets dans la région, a été construite en 2005. Suivant les instructions de ses propriétaires, elle est entièrement bâtie en bois et en verre et dispose d'un espace suffisant pour accueillir non seulement la famille, mais aussi les amis. Toutes les chambres sont de dimensions identiques, ce qui facilite l'organisation, d'après la maîtresse de maison. Un autre détail intéressant est la forme de la terrasse, qui permet de changer d'endroit pour prendre les repas, selon l'envie.

LEFT ABOVE:
The little gate opens from the swimming pool to the beach. The outdoor area affords numerous shady corners ideal for rest or reading.

LEFT BELOW:
The small flight of steps leads to the terrace, which commands a dazzling 180-degree view of the entire beach.

RIGHT:
Another wooden bridge crosses a small lake, which runs under the coconut grove from the house to the poolside deck.

LINKS OBEN:
Durch das kleine Holztor geht es vom Swimmingpool zum Strand. Im Garten gibt es viele schattige Plätze, die zum Ausruhen oder Lesen einladen.

LINKS UNTEN:
Die kurze Treppe führt zu einer Aussichtsterrasse, von der aus man einen Rundumblick auf den ganzen Strand hat.

RECHTE SEITE:
Ein weiterer Holzsteg führt vom Haus über einen kleinen Teich zum Swimmingpool, der von Kokospalmen beschattet wird.

À GAUCHE, EN HAUT :
Un petit portail permet d'accéder à la plage depuis la piscine. Plusieurs coins ombragés aménagés autour de la maison sont parfaits pour le repos ou la lecture.

À GAUCHE, EN BAS :
Une volée de marches mène à la terrasse, d'où l'on peut admirer le panorama éblouissant de la plage.

PAGE DE DROITE :
Un autre pont en bois traverse l'étang entre la maison et la passerelle au bord de la piscine, sous les cocotiers.

CASA SAN MARCO / TRANCOSO

LEFT:
The natural landscape, which is set off by the small lake at the front of the house, comprises coconut palms and native vegetation.

RIGHT ABOVE AND BELOW:
The wooden furniture with white upholstery strikes a note of simplicity appropriate for a house by the sea.

LINKE SEITE:
Kokospalmen und andere einheimische Pflanzen wachsen im Garten, dessen Natürlichkeit durch den Teich vor dem Haus akzentuiert wird.

RECHTS OBEN UND UNTEN:
Die weiß gepolsterten Holzmöbel vermitteln in ihrer Schlichtheit ein für ein Haus am Strand typisches einfaches Leben.

PAGE DE GAUCHE :
Les cocotiers et les plantes indigènes composent l'aspect naturel du paysage, renforcé par l'étang devant la maison.

À DROITE, EN HAUT ET EN BAS :
Les meubles en bois et les coussins blancs créent l'atmosphère de dépouillement nécessaire à une maison au bord de la mer.

CASA SAN MARCO / TRANCOSO

Casa do Quadrado

FERNANDO DROGHETTI

TRANCOSO

Trancoso is considered to be one of the oldest Jesuit villages in the world. The arrival in Brazil of the first religious followers of the Society of Jesus, founded by St Ignatius of Loyola in the 16th century, came shortly after the discovery of Brazil in 1500. The humble cluster of houses around the rectangular town square, with the church of St John the Baptist at one end with its back to the sea, was built by the Jesuits around 1586. Since the 1970s, when the first hippies began to arrive in Trancoso, the Praça de São João Batista (the Square of St John the Baptist) has been known as the "Quadrado" or "Square". It is the nerve centre of everything that happens in the village, so its uniform, colourful houses have become sought-after and prized not only as homes but also as designer shops, restaurants and inns. One of the privileged few to have a house in the Quadrado is Fernando Droghetti, a São Paulo interior decoration entrepreneur who, with the help of architect Sig Bergamin, lent a distinctly Brazilian charm to the décor.

LEFT PAGE:
The outside corridor leads to the rooms and a stretch of land which sweeps down to the Trancoso River, next to the sea.

LEFT:
As the houses are listed by the foundation that administers the "Quadrilátero do Descobrimento" (Discovery Square), the only modification that may be made to the façades is to paint them a different colour.

LINKE SEITE:
Der Durchgang führt zu den Zimmern und zum Garten, der bis an den Fluss Trancoso und das Meeresufer reicht.

LINKS:
Der Häuserkomplex am Quadrado steht unter Denkmalschutz, daher dürfen die Fassaden der Häuser nicht substanziell verändert, sondern lediglich neu gestrichen werden.

PAGE DE GAUCHE :
Le passage extérieur mène aux chambres à coucher ainsi qu'à une parcelle de terrain qui descend jusqu'au fleuve Trancoso, en bord de mer.

À GAUCHE :
Comme ce quartier est placé sous la protection de la fondation qui administre le Quadrilátero do Descobrimento, la seule modification possible sur les façades est d'en changer la couleur.

Trancoso gilt als eine der ältesten Jesuitensiedlungen der Welt. Die ersten Jesuiten, deren Orden von Ignatius von Loyola Anfang des 16. Jahrhunderts gegründet wurde, gelangten bereits kurz nach der Entdeckung Brasiliens im Jahre 1500 hierher. Um 1586 legten sie rings um einen rechteckigen, grünen Platz einen Häuserkomplex mit der vom Meer abgewandten Kirche São João Batista an. Als die ersten Hippies in den 1970er-Jahren nach Trancoso kamen, wurde der Platz, der vormals den Namen São João Batista trug, in Quadrado („Quadrat") umbenannt. Hier laufen alle Stränge des Dorflebens zusammen. Die gleichförmigen, bunten Häuschen rund um den Platz sind heutzutage sehr gefragt und sorgen für steigende Grundstückspreise. Sie beherbergen nicht nur Privatwohnungen, sondern auch elegante Boutiquen, Restaurants und Hotels. Einer der Privilegierten, der ein Haus am Quadrado besitzt, ist der Unternehmer Fernando Droghetti aus São Paulo. Mithilfe des Architekten Sig Bergamin hat er seinem Haus brasilianischen Charme verliehen.

Trancoso est considérée comme l'une des plus vieilles bourgades jésuites du monde. L'arrivée au Brésil des premiers religieux de la compagnie de Jésus, fondée par Ignace de Loyola au XVIᵉ siècle, a eu lieu peu après la découverte du Brésil, en l'an 1500. Un ensemble de maisons simples entourent la place rectangulaire couverte de gazon, au fond de laquelle se dresse l'église São João Batista, édifiée autour de 1586 et qui surplombe la mer. C'est depuis les années 70, lorsque les premiers hippies sont arrivés à Trancoso, que la place São João Batista est connue sous le nom de « Quadrado ». C'est là le lieu de convergence de la vie du hameau, ce qui a fini par rendre ces petites maisons identiques et colorées très recherchées. Aujourd'hui, elles ont été transformées en résidences, boutiques de marque, restaurants ou auberges. L'entrepreneur en décoration Fernando Droghetti, de São Paulo, est l'un des privilégiés possédant une maison sur le Quadrado. Avec l'aide de l'architecte Sig Bergamin, il a donné à la décoration un charme très brésilien.

LEFT ABOVE:
At the entrance to the house is an old wardrobe from Minas Gerais now used as a crockery cupboard. The plaque reading '0045' on the wall, probably from a boat, was found on the beach.

LEFT BELOW:
The twin saints Cosmas and Damian are a painted plaster lamp. The stand is made of wire and glass.

RIGHT:
The dining table came from a ranch in Minas Gerais, and the chairs were purchased in São Paulo. The wooden wall sconce was found in Trancoso.

LINKS OBEN:
Im Eingangsbereich steht ein alter Schrank aus Minas Gerais, in dem Geschirr aufbewahrt wird. Das als Strandgut angeschwemmte Schild „0045" stammt vermutlich von einem Boot.

LINKS UNTEN:
Die Heiligen Kosmas und Damian sind eine Lampe aus Gips. Der Tisch darunter ist aus Draht und Glas gefertigt.

RECHTE SEITE:
Der Esstisch stammt von einer Fazenda in Minas Gerais, die Stühle kommen aus São Paulo. Die hölzerne Wandleuchte ist eine Arbeit aus Trancoso.

À GAUCHE, EN HAUT :
Dans l'entrée de la maison, une armoire typique du Minas Gerais. La plaque « 0045 », provenant vraisemblablement d'un bateau, a été trouvée sur la plage.

À GAUCHE, EN BAS :
La statue des saints jumeaux Côme et Damien, est un luminaire en plâtre peint. Le support est en fil de fer et en verre.

PAGE DE DROITE :
La table servant aux repas provient d'une ferme du Minas Gerais et les chaises ont été dénichées à São Paulo. Sur le mur, une applique en bois venant de Trancoso.

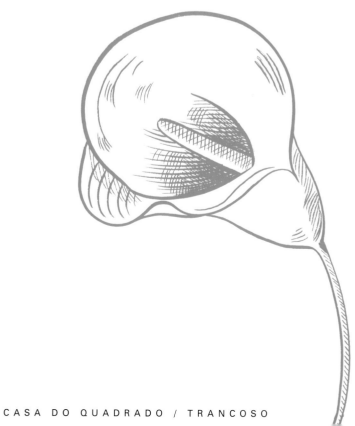

CASA DO QUADRADO / TRANCOSO

LEFT PAGE:
In the living room, the collection of indigenous head-dresses was framed and turned into a work of art. The table in the centre is an antique from Sul da Bahia.

RIGHT PAGE:
The armchair and the pouffes in the living room were handmade in Trancoso from taboa, a fibre very common in the region. Next to the cupboard is a wooden Thai bell.

LINKE SEITE:
Der gerahmte indianische Federschmuck ist Teil des Wohnzimmerszenarios. Der antike Tisch in der Mitte kommt aus dem Süden Bahias.

RECHTE SEITE:
Der Sessel und die Puffs im Wohnzimmer wurden in Trancoso aus taboa-Fasern gefertigt. Neben dem Schrank hängt eine thailändische Holzglocke.

PAGE DE GAUCHE :
Dans la pièce principale, la collection de parures indigènes a été encadrée et s'est transformée en œuvre d'art. La table ancienne provient du sud de l'Etat de Bahia.

PAGE DE DROITE :
Dans la pièce principale, le fauteuil et les poufs tressés en taboa, une variété de roseau très commune dans la région, ont été fabriqués à Trancoso. A côté de l'armoire, un gong thaïlandais en bois.

88

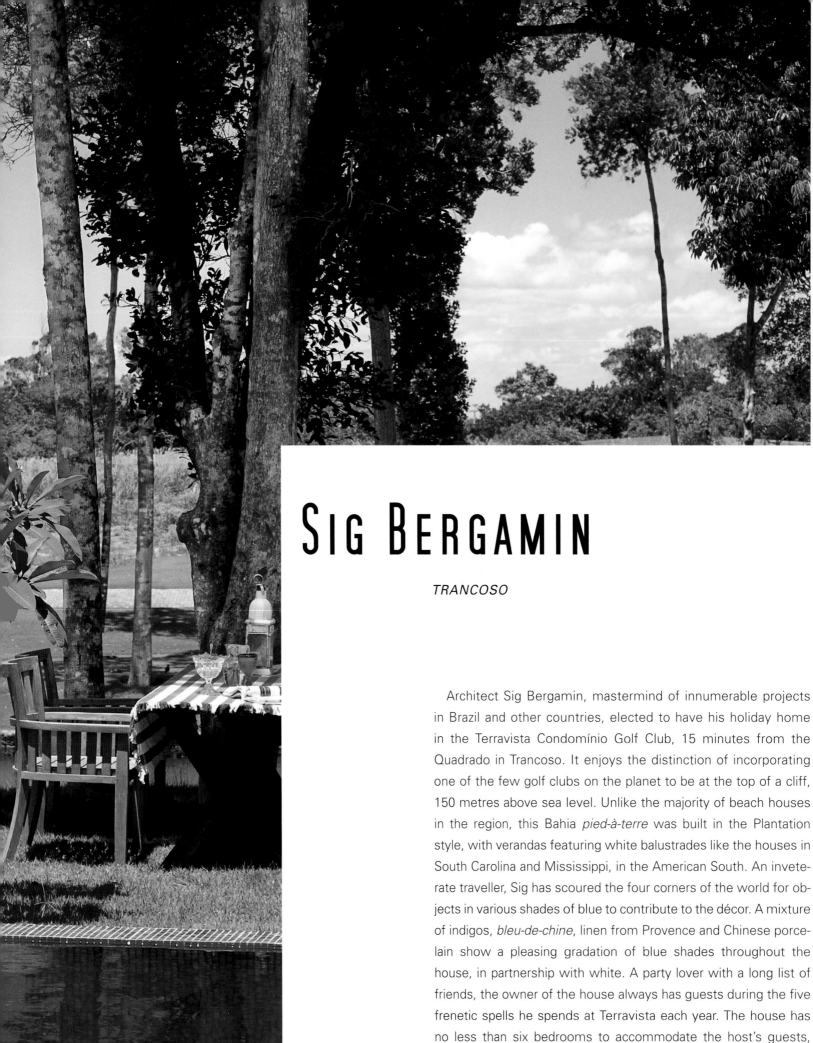

SIG BERGAMIN

TRANCOSO

Architect Sig Bergamin, mastermind of innumerable projects in Brazil and other countries, elected to have his holiday home in the Terravista Condomínio Golf Club, 15 minutes from the Quadrado in Trancoso. It enjoys the distinction of incorporating one of the few golf clubs on the planet to be at the top of a cliff, 150 metres above sea level. Unlike the majority of beach houses in the region, this Bahia *pied-à-terre* was built in the Plantation style, with verandas featuring white balustrades like the houses in South Carolina and Mississippi, in the American South. An invete-rate traveller, Sig has scoured the four corners of the world for ob-jects in various shades of blue to contribute to the décor. A mixture of indigos, *bleu-de-chine*, linen from Provence and Chinese porce-lain show a pleasing gradation of blue shades throughout the house, in partnership with white. A party lover with a long list of friends, the owner of the house always has guests during the five frenetic spells he spends at Terravista each year. The house has no less than six bedrooms to accommodate the host's guests, who are provided with every comfort.

LEFT PAGE:
In the late afternoon, the host and his guests meet for tea by the pool, under the shade of the trees.

RIGHT:
In Plantation-style houses, as in the American South, the usual architectural layout is reversed: entertaining spaces are on the upper floor and private quarters on the lower floor.

LINKE SEITE:
An den Nachmittagen treffen sich der Gastgeber und seine Besucher im Schatten der Bäume zu einem Tee am Swimmingpool.

RECHTS:
Die Raumanordnung folgt der amerikanischen Südstaatentradition: Das Obergeschoss ist den Gästen vorbehalten, die privaten Räume befinden sich unten.

PAGE DE GAUCHE :
En fin d'après-midi, l'hôte et ses invités aiment se retrouver pour le thé à l'ombre des arbres, au bord de la piscine.

À DROITE :
Dans le style « plantation » des maisons du sud des Etats-Unis, les règles architectoniques ont été inversées : la partie ouverte aux invités se trouve à l'étage et l'espace privé au rez-de-chaussée.

91

Sig Bergamin, Architekt zahlloser Projekte in Brasilien und anderen Ländern, hat sich für sein Sommerhaus den eleganten „Terravista Condomínio Golf Club" ausgesucht, einen geschlossenen Wohnbezirk, nur 15 Minuten vom Zentrum Trancosos entfernt und mit einem der wenigen Golfplätze weltweit, die auf einer Steilküste 150 Meter über dem Meer liegen. In Gegensatz zu den meisten anderen Küstenhäusern dieser Gegend beschloss Bergamin, sein Ferienhaus in Bahia im Südstaatenstil zu bauen: Die Veranden mit weißen Balustraden erinnern an die Villen auf Plantagen in Mississippi oder South Carolina. Die Einrichtung des Hauses ist von Objekten in Blautönen bestimmt, die der rastlose Sig Bergamin in allen vier Erdteilen gesammelt hat. Eine Mischung von Indigos, *bleu-de-chine*, provenzalischem Leinen und chinesischem Porzellan bildet eine subtile Blaupalette, die mit dem allgegenwärtigen Weiß im Haus harmoniert. Der Hausherr, der gerne häufig Feste feiert und einen großen Freundeskreis hat, empfängt immer Gäste im Terravista. Die sechs Gästezimmer des Hauses, in denen der Hausherr seinen Besuchern allen erdenklichen Komfort bietet, waren daher ein absolutes Muss.

Auteur de nombreux projets au Brésil et dans d'autres pays, l'architecte Sig Bergamin a choisi de construire sa résidence d'été dans l'élégante copropriété du terrain de golf Terravista Condomínio, à 15 minutes du « Quadrado » de Trancoso. Ce golf est l'un des rares au monde situé sur une falaise, à 150 mètres au-dessus de la mer. Contrairement à la plupart des propriétaires des maisons situées en bord de mer dans la région, Sig Bergamin a adopté le style « plantation », avec des terrasses aux balustrades blanches, à l'image des maisons de Caroline du Sud et du Mississippi. Voyageur invétéré, il a déniché des objets dans différents tons de bleu aux quatre coins du monde pour composer la décoration. Le mélange des indigos, du bleu de Chine, des tissus en lin de Provence et des porcelaines chinoises forme un agréable dégradé de bleu qui, avec le blanc, est présent dans toute la maison. Le maître de maison, amateur de fêtes et possédant de nombreux amis, est toujours entouré au cours des cinq séjours animés qu'il passe chaque année à Terravista. Les six chambres à coucher de la maison ne sont pas de trop pour recevoir les invités, avec toute l'attention dont cet amateur de réceptions aime les entourer.

LEFT ABOVE:
Ever favouring shades of blue, the architect lined the swimming pool with deep blue tiles, mirroring the sky.

LEFT BELOW:
The twin shell-shaped consoles in the spacious blue and white living room were sourced at Christie's.

RIGHT ABOVE AND BELOW:
Natural fibres, such as the rattan in the veranda tables and chairs, have also fallen victim to the house owner's blue mania. The orchids on the table were grown in the garden.

LINKE SEITE OBEN:
Der Architekt kleidete den Swimmingpool mit Kacheln in einem von ihm bevorzugten tiefen Blauton aus und machte ihn damit zu einem „Spiegel" des Himmels.

LINKE SEITE UNTEN:
Die muschelförmigen Konsolen im blau-weißen Wohnzimmer wurden bei Christie's ersteigert.

RECHTS OBEN UND UNTEN:
Auch die Stühle und Tische auf der Veranda entsprechen der Vorliebe des Hausherrn für die Farbe Blau. Die Orchideen stammen aus dem eigenen Garten.

PAGE DE GAUCHE, EN HAUT :
Privilégiant les tons bleus, l'architecte a recouvert le fond de la piscine de petits carreaux d'un bleu profond, offrant ainsi un miroir au ciel.

PAGE DE GAUCHE, EN BAS :
Dans le vaste salon bleu et blanc, la paire de consoles en forme de coquillage vient de chez Christie's.

À DROITE, EN HAUT ET EN BAS :
La passion du maître de maison pour le bleu se retrouve aussi dans les tables et les chaises en osier de la terrasse. Les orchidées posées sur la table viennent du jardin.

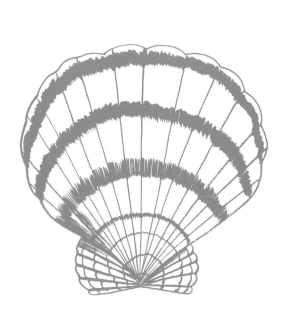

SIG BERGAMIN / TRANCOSO

LEFT:
In the corner next to the stairs everything has a maritime theme, from the coral on the table with sculptures depicting fish to the paintings and the chair with a shell-shaped backrest.

RIGHT ABOVE:
The hallway, which leads to the dining room on the ground floor, features native banana trees planted in vases acquired in Vietnam.

RIGHT BELOW:
Sig Bergamin likes to mix framed engravings on paper together with photographs in the same space. The picture with the circle and stars depicts the middle of the Brazilian flag.

LINKE SEITE:
Alle Gegenstände neben der Treppe verweisen auf das Meer: von den Korallen auf dem mit Fischen verzierten Tisch bis zu den Wandbildern und dem muschelförmigen Stuhl.

RECHTS OBEN:
Die einheimischen Bananenpalmen in Töpfen aus Vietnam stehen im Erdgeschoss, im Entree zum Speisezimmer.

RECHTS UNTEN:
Sig Bergamin kombiniert gern Kunstdrucke mit Fotografien. Die Abbildung des blauen Kreises mit Sternen ist ein Element der brasilianischen Fahne.

PAGE DE GAUCHE :
Dans le coin, en bas de l'escalier, tout fait référence à la mer : les coraux sur la table ornée de sculptures de poissons, les tableaux et la chaise au dossier en forme de coquillage.

À DROITE, EN HAUT :
Le hall d'entrée, qui mène à la salle à manger au rez-de-chaussée, est agrémenté de bananiers plantés dans des vases rapportés du Vietnam.

À DROITE, EN BAS :
Sig Bergamin aime mélanger tableaux, gravures et photographies au sein d'une même atmosphère. Le disque bleu avec des étoiles est la partie centrale du drapeau brésilien.

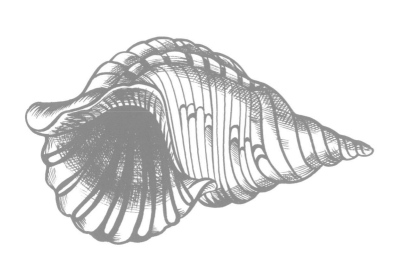

SIG BERGAMIN / TRANCOSO

In the large blue living room
the gate-leg table dates
from the 19th century. The
two chairs are upholstered
with fabric from linen sacks
that used to contain flour.
The sacks were purchased
from an antique shop in
Provence.

Der Gateleg-Tisch im blauen
Salon stammt aus dem 19.
Jahrhundert. Die Sesselbe-
züge waren ursprünglich
leinene Mehlsäcke, die aus
einem Antiquitätenladen in
der Provence stammen.

Dans le grand salon bleu,
la table à abattants est
du XIXᵉ siècle. Les deux
chaises ont été recouvertes
de sacs en lin, autrefois
utilisés pour conserver la
farine, achetés chez un
antiquaire en Provence.

FAZENDA SANTO ANTÔNIO

DONATA MEIRELLES & NIZAN GUANAES
TRANCOSO

Strange as it may seem, advertising agent Nizan Guanaes started to frequent the southern part of Bahia, the state where he was born, only after he was taken there by friends from São Paulo, the city where he lives and works. With his wife, fashion entrepreneur Donata Meirelles, he grew attached to Trancoso, first as a guest at hotels in the village and later as the owner of a charming house on Itapororoca beach, located between Trancoso and Praia do Espelho das Maravilhas beach. To make his seaside *pied-à-terre* a reality, he gathered a team of professionals who were well acquainted with the region: builder Ricardo Salem and architect Beatriz Régis Bittencourt were responsible for the architectural aspects of the project, architect Sig Bergamin created the interior design and landscape artist Isabel Duprat styled the greenery. Christened "Fazenda Santo Antônio" (St Anthony Ranch), after Nizan's preferred saint as well as the name of his son, the owners' only stipulation was that it be built on stilts for ventilation, and that it command a view of the sea from every angle.

99

So verwunderlich es auch klingen mag, der in Bahia geborene Werbefachmann Nizan Guanaes hat die Südküste seines Geburtsortes erst zusammen mit Freunden aus São Paulo, der Stadt in der er lebt und arbeitet, wiederentdeckt. Er und seine Frau Donata Meirelles, eine Modeunternehmerin, entwickelten zuerst als Hotelgäste eine Verbundenheit zu Trancoso, später als Hausbesitzer am Itapororoca-Strand, der zwischen Trancoso und Praia do Espelho das Maravilhas liegt. Um sein Zweithaus an der Küste zu errichten, versammelte Nizan ein Team von Spezialisten, die mit der Region sehr gut vertraut sind: den Bauunternehmer Ricardo Salem und die Architektin Beatriz Régis Bittencourt für das Bauprojekt, den Architekten Sig Bergamin für die Inneneinrichtung und die Landschaftsarchitektin Isabel Duprat für die Gartengestaltung. Das Haus wurde „Fazenda Santo Antônio" getauft und trägt damit den Namen des Schutzheiligen Nizans, der auch der Namenspatron seines Sohnes ist. Die Hauseigentümer wünschten sich nur, dass das Haus auf Pfählen erbaut wird und nach allen Seiten Meeresblick hat.

Aussi curieux que cela puisse paraître, c'est grâce à des amis de São Paulo, où il vit et travaille, que le publicitaire Nizan Guanaes a commencé à découvrir le sud de sa région natale. Avec son épouse, Donata Meirelles, chef d'entreprise dans le secteur de la mode, il a d'abord fait connaissance avec Trancoso en séjournant dans les hôtels du hameau, pour finir propriétaire d'une charmante maison située sur la plage d'Itapororoca, entre Trancoso et Praia do Espelho das Maravilhas. Pour donner vie à ce pied-à-terre en bord de mer, il a fait appel à une équipe de professionnels habitués de la région : Ricardo Salem et Beatriz Régis Bittencourt pour la partie architectonique du projet, l'architecte Sig Bergamin pour la décoration intérieure et la paysagiste Isabel Duprat pour les espaces verts. Par dévotion à saint Antoine, qui est aussi le prénom de son fils, Nizan Guanaes a baptisé sa maison Fazenda Santo Antônio. La seule exigence qu'il a exprimée a été de construire la maison sur pilotis afin de bénéficier d'une ventilation optimale et d'une excellente vue sur la mer.

LEFT PAGE:
Collectors of ethnic art, the couple juxtapose African and indigenous items, along with images such as the twin saints Cosmas and Damian, and the Afro-Brazilian religious entity Xangô.

RIGHT PAGE:
The table seats 12 but is hardly big enough for the lunches and dinners the couple throw for their friends, as they never invite fewer than 20.

LINKE SEITE:
In der Sammlung ethnischer Kunstgegenstände vermischen sich afrikanische und indianische Objekte, darunter die Heiligen Kosmas und Damian sowie Xangô, eine afro-brasilianische Gottheit.

RECHTE SEITE:
Der lange Tisch für zwölf Personen ist eigentlich immer zu klein, denn das Ehepaar bewirtet selten weniger als zwanzig Gäste.

PAGE DE GAUCHE :
Collectionneur d'art ethnique, le couple mélange les objets africains et indigènes et les statues, comme celles des saints jumeaux Côme et Damien et celle de Xangô, une divinité afro-brésilienne.

100

PAGE DE DROITE :
La table pour douze personnes paraît bien petite lors des repas que le couple a l'habitude d'organiser pour les amis, et auxquels participent toujours au moins une vingtaine d'invités.

LEFT:
The living room, with its symmetrical arrangement of armchairs and sofas (a trademark of Sig Bergamin), emphasises natural fibre and local handicrafts.

RIGHT ABOVE:
In addition to the master bedroom, there are three further bedrooms.

RIGHT BELOW:
A fashion addict, in her private bathroom Donata has hung a painting with depictions of Chanel No. 5 perfume bottles and a tin sculpture of a dress bought in Trancoso.

LINKE SEITE:
Im Wohnzimmer, dessen symmetrische Möbelanordnung die Handschrift Sig Bergamins trägt, dominieren Naturfasern und lokales Kunsthandwerk.

RECHTS OBEN:
Außer dem Schlafzimmer des Ehepaares gibt es noch drei weitere Schlafzimmer im Haus.

RECHTS UNTEN:
In ihrem privaten Badezimmer stellt die Modeliebhaberin Donata ein Kunstwerk mit Chanel-Parfüms und eine metallene Kleidskulptur aus Trancoso zur Schau.

PAGE DE GAUCHE :
Le living, avec la disposition symétrique des fauteuils et des canapés (caractéristique de Sig Bergamin), met en valeur les fibres naturelles et l'artisanat local.

À DROITE, EN HAUT :
En plus de celle du couple, la maison possède trois chambres.

À DROITE, EN BAS :
Dans sa salle de bains personnelle, Donata Meirelles, passionnée de mode, a placé un cadre reproduisant des flacons de Chanel n°5 et une sculpture de vêtement réalisée à partir de boîtes de conserve, achetée à Trancoso.

FAZENDA SANTO ANTÔNIO / TRANCOSO

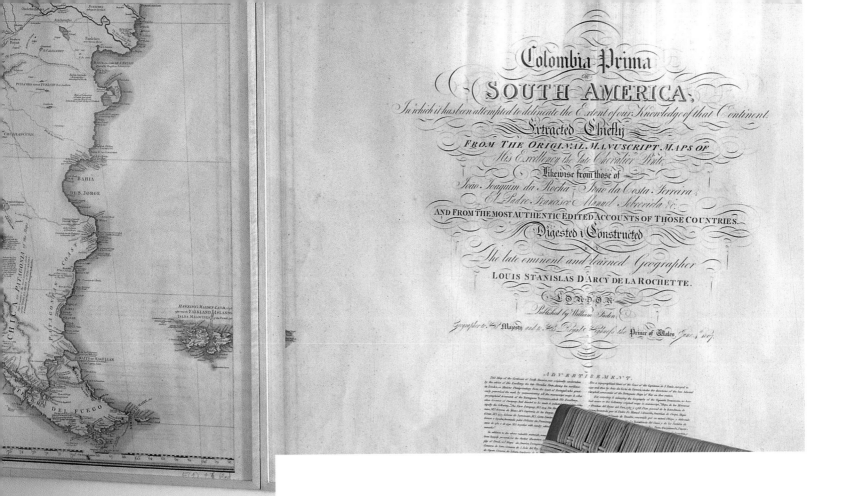

CASA DO PICCHIO

OUTEIRO DAS BRISAS

Outeiro das Brisas, one of the most exclusive areas in Sul da Bahia, is located on the clifftops with views over beautiful Espelho das Maravilhas beach, which stretches between the villages of Trancoso and Caraíva. In 1987, the owner of Casa do Picchio, a European who divides his time between Switzerland, London and New York, was introduced to the area by a friend. He instantly fell in love with it and decided he would build his dream house there. The house was built between 1992 and 1994 by Ricardo Salem, an outstandig builder from the Trancoso region. Salem followed the owner's instructions, in particular the "crazy idea" of building the house of wood and glass only, echoing the architecture of local houses but on a far larger scale. The use of wood suggested the choice of name for the house, Picchio, which is the Italian word for the woodpecker. Because of their peripatetic lifestyle, moving between the cities where they have residences, the family are able to enjoy the house for only two weeks each year, usually around the time of the end-of-year festivities. However, the house is always available to their friends and their eldest daughter, who lives in New York.

LEFT PAGE AND RIGHT:
The map of South America is rare, dating from the late 18th or early 19th century. It was bought in a second-hand bookshop in Beauchamp Place, London.

LINKE SEITE UND RECHTS:
Die Südamerikakarte ist eine Rarität und stammt vom Ende des 18., Anfang des 19. Jahrhunderts. Sie wurde bei einem Antiquar in Beauchamp Place, London gekauft.

PAGE DE GAUCHE ET À DROITE :
La carte de l'Amérique du Sud, une pièce rare de la fin du XVIIIe siècle ou du début du XIXe siècle, a été achetée chez un antiquaire de Beauchamp Place, à Londres.

Outeiro das Brisas, eine exklusive Gegend zwischen Trancoso und Caraíva, liegt auf einer Steilküste, von der man auf den wunderschönen Strand Espelho das Maravilhas blickt. Der Besitzer der Casa do Picchio, ein Europäer, der zwischen der Schweiz, London und New York pendelt, lernte den Ort 1987 durch einen Freund kennen. Es war Liebe auf den ersten Blick, und er beschloss, hier sein Traumhaus zu errichten. Gebaut wurde es 1992 bis 1994 von Ricardo Salem, dem bekannten Bauherrn der Region Trancoso. Der Hausbesitzer wollte das Haus in Anlehnung an die lokale Bauweise, allerdings in wesentlich größerem Stil, nur aus Holz und Glas errichten. Die Dominanz von Holz war auch bestimmend für die Namensgebung des Hauses: *picchio*, italienisch für Specht. Nur rund zwei Wochen im Jahr, meistens um die Jahreswende, verbringt die Familie, die das ganze Jahr zwischen ihren unterschiedlichen Wohnsitzen pendelt, in diesem Haus. Es steht jedoch Freunden immer offen und wird auch häufiger von der älteren Tochter genutzt, die in New York wohnt.

L'un des endroits les plus remarquables du sud de l'Etat de Bahia, Outeiro das Brisas, est situé sur la partie haute de la falaise d'où se dévoile la magnifique plage d'Espelho das Maravilhas, entre les hameaux de Trancoso et Caraíva. En 1987, le futur propriétaire de la Casa do Picchio, un Européen vivant entre la Suisse, Londres et New York, a été amené par un ami dans cet endroit dont il est tombé amoureux, au point de décider d'y avoir la « maison de ses rêves ». Celle-ci a été construite par Ricardo Salem (maître d'ouvrage de la région de Trancoso) entre 1992 et 1994, en suivant les instructions de son propriétaire, que celui-ci qualifie « d'idée folle » et qui consistait à réaliser une maison uniquement en bois et en verre, en respectant l'architecture locale mais en voyant beaucoup plus grand. L'utilisation du bois a inspiré le nom de la maison, Picchio, qui en italien signifie pic-vert, cet oiseau qui cogne les troncs d'arbre de son bec. Menant une vie mouvementée entre plusieurs villes, la famille ne passe que deux semaines par an ici, généralement pendant les fêtes de fin d'année, mais la maison est toujours ouverte pour les amis ainsi que pour leur fille aînée qui vit à New York.

LEFT:
*One of the highlights of the
house is the trompe l'œil
on the lobby wall by the
entrance, painted by French
artist Pascal Rochette. It
depicts the flora and fauna
of the Atlantic Forest.*

RIGHT ABOVE:
*To the right of the main
lobby is a chest of drawers,
originally from a Brazilian
ranch. It was bought in an
antique shop in São Paulo,
as was the bench by
the wall adorned with the
trompe l'œil.*

RIGHT BELOW:
*Detail of a painting featuring
bromeliads and a small
monkey known as a mico.*

LINKE SEITE:
*Einer der Blickfänge des
Hauses ist die trompe-l'œil-
Malerei des Franzosen Pas-
cal Rochette an einer Wand
am Eingang. Sie stellt die
Flora und Fauna des Atlanti-
schen Regenwaldes dar.*

RECHTS OBEN:
*Die Kommode im Fazenda-
stil rechts in der Eingangs-
halle und die Bank vor der
trompe-l'œil-Malerei wur-
den in einem Antiquitäten-
geschäft in São Paulo
gekauft.*

RECHTS UNTEN:
*Ein Ausschnitt der Wand-
malerei zeigt Bromelien
und ein Kapuzineräffchen.*

PAGE DE GAUCHE :
*Une des singularités de la
maison est le trompe-l'œil,
peint par l'artiste français
Pascal Rochette, sur le mur
du hall d'entrée, qui représente la faune et la flore
de la forêt du littoral.*

À DROITE, EN HAUT :
*Sur la droite du hall d'entrée
se trouve une commode
achetée chez un antiquaire
de São Paulo. Elle provient
d'une ferme brésilienne,
tout comme le banc placé
devant le mur en trompe-
l'œil.*

À DROITE, EN BAS :
*Un détail de la peinture, où
l'on peut voir des broméliacées et un petit singe mico.*

CASA DO PICCHIO / OUTEIRO DAS BRISAS

LEFT ABOVE:
The lush vegetation can be seen through the doors and windows, which are made of local glass and wood.

LEFT BELOW:
In the heart of Sul da Bahia, in a house typical of the region, there is yet a touch of Europe, courtesy of the old stool at the foot of the bed in the main suite.

RIGHT:
The golden glow of late afternoon enters the house, where rustic wood and ceramic floor blend harmoniously with the modern Italian high-tech light fittings.

LINKS OBEN:
Durch Fenster und Türen aus Holz und Glas sieht man üppiges Grün.

LINKS UNTEN:
Die antike Sitzbank vor dem Bett verleiht dem im traditionellen Stil des Südens von Bahia eingerichteten Haus einen europäischen Touch.

RECHTE SEITE:
Goldenes Nachmittagslicht dringt in das Haus, in dem sich rustikale Holzelemente und der Keramikboden perfekt mit den modernen italienischen Designleuchten vertragen.

À GAUCHE, EN HAUT :
L'ambiance de la végétation luxuriante envahit la maison par les portes-fenêtres vitrées, fabriquées en bois de la région.

À GAUCHE, EN BAS :
En plein sud de l'Etat de Bahia, dans une maison au style typique, le vieux banc au pied du lit apporte une « touche européenne ».

PAGE DE DROITE :
En fin d'après-midi, la lumière dorée pénètre dans la maison, où le bois rustique et le sol en céramique cohabitent harmonieusement avec les luminaires modernes « high-tech » de style italien.

CASA DO PICCHIO / OUTEIRO DAS BRISAS

Carla & Tuca Reinés

VILA DO OUTEIRO

Photographer and architect Tuca Reinés designed his own house in Vila do Outeiro, which occupies a heavenly spot atop a cliff located between Trancoso and the village of Caraíva, overlooking Espelho das Maravilhas beach. The wooden house was inspired by the fishermen's houses in Sul da Bahia. Tuca, Carla and the children, Georgia and Eric, love nature and the outdoors. The family live in São Paulo but they take long holidays by the sea, where Tuca indulges in simple pastimes that are impossible in the big city, such as undersea fishing, cooking on a wood stove or taking long walks on the beach. The house accommodates the diverse collections of objects that they have amassed from their travels around the world and, in particular, anything that the sea brings forth, be it seashells or coral, whelks or stones. The house has only two bedrooms, one for the parents and one for the children. The furniture, which emphasises straight lines, was designed by Carla and built by local carpenters.

111

Der Fotograf und Architekt Tuca Reinés entwarf sein Haus in Vila do Outeiro selbst, einem paradiesischen, auf einer Steilküste zwischen Trancoso und dem Dorf Caraíva gelegenen Ort. Von hier aus schaut man direkt auf den Strand Espelho das Maravilhas. Das Holzhaus wurde von den Fischerhäusern im Süden Bahias inspiriert und zeugt auch vom Wunsch der Besitzer nach Einfachheit. Alle in der Familie, bestehend aus Tuca, Carla und den Kindern Georgia und Eric, lieben die Natur und das Leben im Freien. Die Familie lebt eigentlich in São Paulo, verbringt aber lange Urlaube an der Küste, wo Tuca den Vergnügungen nachgehen kann, die in der Großstadt nicht möglich sind: Unterwasserjagd, Kochen am mit Holz befeuertem Herd oder lange Spaziergänge am Strand. Das Haus beherbergt Reisesouvenirs der Familie sowie Dinge, die das Meer heranträgt: verschiedene Muschelarten, Korallen, Steine. Im Haus gibt es lediglich zwei Schlafzimmer: eines für das Ehepaar und eines für die Kinder. Die von Carla entworfene und von lokalen Schreinern gefertigte Einrichtung zeichnet sich vor allem durch ihre Gradlinigkeit aus.

Photographe et architecte, Tuca Reinés a conçu sa propre maison à Vila do Outeiro, lieu paradisiaque situé entre Trancoso et le hameau de Caraíva, en haut d'une falaise dominant la plage d'Espelho das Maravilhas. La maison en bois est inspirée des maisons de pêcheurs du sud de l'Etat de Bahia et reflète la manière de vivre de Tuca Reinés, Carla et leurs enfants Georgia et Eric, amoureux de la nature et de la vie au grand air. La famille habite à São Paulo mais passe ses vacances au bord de la mer, où Tuca Reinés s'adonne à des activités simples, impossibles à pratiquer dans la métropole, telles que la pêche sous-marine, la cuisine au feu de bois ou les longues promenades sur la plage. La maison abrite diverses collections d'objets que la famille déniche au cours de ses voyages à travers le monde et en particulier des objets apportés par la mer : coquillages, coraux ou cailloux. La maison possède seulement deux chambres à coucher, celle des parents et celle des enfants, et est garnie de mobilier aux lignes droites, dessiné par Carla et réalisé par des menuisiers de la région.

LEFT:
The tree in front of the house, an ingazeira, grew after a child played in the garden with the seed of the fruit, not meaning to plant it.

RIGHT ABOVE:
The bungalow is in the lower part of the house, and its veranda serves as a dining room. The enclosed area is used for storage.

RIGHT BELOW:
The barbecue is made entirely of round stones, like those used to frame the front of the house.

LINKE SEITE:
Der Baum vor dem Haus, eine ingazeira, ist überraschenderweise aus einem von den Kindern achtlos in den Garten geworfenen Fruchtkern gewachsen.

RECHTS OBEN:
Die Veranda des unteren Hausbereiches dient als Essplatz, die geschlossenen Räume dahinter als Stauraum.

RECHTS UNTEN:
Der Grillplatz ist mit den gleichen runden Steinen gestaltet, die auch die Hausfront verkleiden.

PAGE DE GAUCHE :
Un noyau de fruit d'ingazeira, jeté au hasard par un enfant, a donné naissance à cet arbre qui a curieusement poussé devant la maison.

À DROITE, EN HAUT :
Le bungalow est situé dans la partie inférieure de la maison et sa terrasse sert de salle à manger. La partie fermée fait office de remise.

À DROITE, EN BAS :
Le barbecue est entièrement construit en pierre ronde, tout comme la façade de la maison.

CARLA & TUCA REINÉS / VILA DO OUTEIRO

LEFT ABOVE:
Grilled sea urchin is a delicious speciality of Tuca, who loves to cook.

LEFT BELOW AND RIGHT:
The dining room on the bungalow veranda houses the collections of "gifts" of the sea: stones, fossils, coral and seashells.

LINKS OBEN:
Gegrillte Seeigel sind eine kulinarische Spezialität Tucas, der ein leidenschaftlicher Koch ist.

LINKS UNTEN UND RECHTE SEITE:
Im offenen Essbereich sind „Geschenke" des Meeres ausgestellt: Treibgut, Steine, Fossilien, Korallen, Muscheln.

À GAUCHE, EN HAUT :
Les oursins cuits à la braise sont une délicieuse spécialité de Tuca qui adore cuisiner.

À GAUCHE, EN BAS, ET PAGE DE DROITE :
La salle à manger sur la terrasse du bungalow est décorée de « présents » de la mer : cailloux, fossiles, coraux et coquillages.

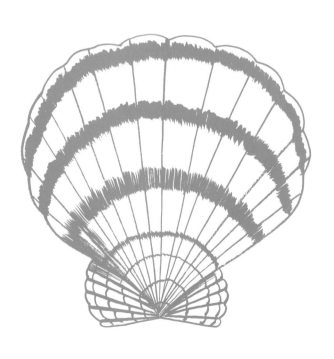

CARLA & TUCA REINÉS / VILA DO OUTEIRO

LEFT ABOVE:
A wonderful view of the sea can be enjoyed from the upper storey.

LEFT BELOW:
Wood from the region is used in the flooring and wall coverings of the living room, which has a sofa-bed big enough for the whole family.

RIGHT:
The sunset suffuses the living room with light. Carla and Tuca used old wooden skis and oars as decorative elements.

LINKS OBEN:
Das Obergeschoss ermöglicht einen spektakulären Blick auf das Meer in der Dämmerung.

LINKS UNTEN:
Lokale Holzarten wurden für die Dielen und die Decken des offenen Wohnbereiches benutzt. Das große Sofa bietet Platz für die ganze Familie.

RECHTE SEITE:
Das Licht des Sonnenuntergangs füllt das Wohnzimmer, das Carla und Tuca mit alten Rudern und Holzskiern dekoriert haben.

À GAUCHE, EN HAUT :
Le coucher de soleil sur la mer s'offre à la vue depuis l'étage supérieur de la maison.

À GAUCHE, EN BAS :
Le living, dont le parquet a été fabriqué avec du bois trouvé dans la région, est meublé d'un canapé-lit pouvant accueillir toute la famille.

PAGE DE DROITE :
La lumière du couchant remplit le living que Carla et Tuca ont décoré de vieilles planches de surf et de rames en bois.

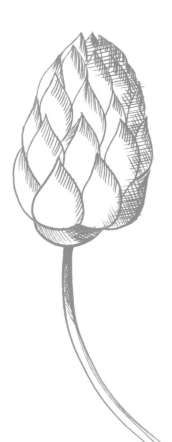

CARLA & TUCA REINÉS / VILA DO OUTEIRO

LEFT AND RIGHT ABOVE:
The old wooden wardrobe is used as a crockery cupboard. On the beam above is a model of a boat used by fishermen in the region.

RIGHT BELOW:
The beach ambiance can be felt in every corner of the house. At the far end is a panel with different sized niches, created by Carla to display her collection of objects.

LINKE SEITE UND RECHTS OBEN:
Der alte Schrank dient zur Aufbewahrung von Geschirr. Auf dem Balken darüber steht das Modell eines einheimischen Fischerboots.

RECHTS UNTEN:
Die Strandatmosphäre ist in allen Ecken des Hauses spürbar. Das Regal für Sammelobjekte aller Art und Größe wurde von Carla entworfen.

PAGE DE GAUCHE ET À DROITE, EN HAUT :
La vieille armoire en bois abrite la vaisselle. Sur la poutre au-dessus se trouve un modèle réduit de barque de pêcheur de la région.

À DROITE, EN BAS :
L'ambiance de la plage est présente dans toute la maison. Au fond, une étagère créée par Carla, avec des niches de différentes tailles pour exposer ses collections.

CARLA & TUCA REINÉS / VILA DO OUTEIRO

LEFT PAGE AND RIGHT PAGE:
The master bedroom is very simple — Carla and Tuca don't need much for their life by the sea. On the floor, a straw mat is used as a rug.

LINKE UND RECHTE SEITE:
Das Ehepaar braucht am Strand nicht viel zum Leben, wovon auch das aufs Wesentliche reduzierte Schlafzimmer zeugt. Eine Strohmatte dient als Teppich.

PAGE DE GAUCHE ET DE DROITE :
La simplicité de la chambre du couple qui a besoin de très peu pour la vie au bord de la mer. Sur le sol, une natte de paille sert de tapis.

The children share a bed-
room, so Tuca placed an
aluminium bowl on a table
to be used as an occasional
washbasin. The sconces
are made of coconut wood.

Die Kinder teilen sich ein
Zimmer. Tuca machte eine
Aluminiumschüssel zum
Waschbecken. Die Wand-
leuchten sind aus Kokosholz
gefertigt.

Dans la chambre des
enfants, Tuca a transformé
en lavabo un bassin en
aluminium sur une table.
Les appliques sont en bois
de cocotier.

122

ISABEL DUPRAT &
MANUEL LEÃO

CURUÍPE

Also known as Praia do Espelho, the little village of Curuípe is south of Trancoso and below Vila do Outeiro. The residents and summer holiday visitors are agreed in not wanting large, luxurious mansions. Rather, there are small fishermen's houses, the charm and good taste of which express their cosmopolitan owners' sense of style. For these individuals, mainly residents of large cities in Brazil, luxury means being able to get up barefoot in the morning, go for walks on the sand and enjoy a long dip in the sea at sunset. That was precisely what landscape gardener Isabel Duprat was looking for when she decided to alternate her work in São Paulo, where she lives, with spells of relaxation and leisure in Praia do Espelho. She made no architectural changes to the small house where she spends the whole summer: there is just one bedroom, a small living room and kitchen, and the bathroom is outside the house, as is common in modest houses in the inland cities. The natural landscape, where almond, coconut and innumerable other Atlantic Forest fruit trees blossom, has gained only the addition of orchids, epidendrums and bromeliads, planted by the lady of the house.

LEFT PAGE:
Mad about flowers, Isabel can't live without them, whether on the table for lunch or in the garden facing the sea.

LEFT :
The concrete flooring dyed with pigment has a cooling effect and is practical for houses on the coastline. The pillars supporting the veranda roof are two tree-trunks.

LINKE SEITE:
Überall wird Isabels Leidenschaft für Blumen deutlich, ob auf dem Mittagstisch oder im Garten, der zum Meer hin liegt.

LINKS:
Der farbige Betonfußboden ist praktisch und wirkt kühlend im heißen Küstenklima. Zwei Baumstämme tragen das Verandadach.

PAGE DE GAUCHE :
Isabel Duprat ne peut pas se passer de fleurs, comme en témoigne la composition sur la table dressée pour le déjeuner, ou le jardin face à la mer.

À GAUCHE :
Le sol, en ciment coloré avec des pigments, est pratique et rafraîchissant. Deux troncs d'arbres soutiennent le toit de la terrasse.

Der Ort Curuípe, auch als Praia do Espelho („Spiegel-Strand") bekannt, liegt südlich von Trancoso und etwas unterhalb von Vila do Outeiro. Einwohner wie auch Sommergäste halten hier nichts von großen Luxusvillen. Dafür zeugen die kleinen Fischerhäuser vom Charme und guten Geschmack ihrer kosmopolitischen Besitzer. Diese, meist aus den riesigen Großstädten Brasiliens kommend, sehen es als Luxus an, morgens barfuß herumzulaufen, am Strand spazieren zu gehen oder bei Sonnenuntergang im Meer zu schwimmen. Genau dies wünschte sich auch die Landschaftsarchitektin Isabel Duprat, als sie sich entschied, die Arbeit in São Paulo, wo sie lebt, durch Momente der Entspannung in Praia do Espelho zu unterbrechen. Sie ließ das kleine Sommerhaus unverändert: Es enthält nur ein Schlafzimmer, ein Wohnzimmer, eine Küche und ein Bad im Freien, wie es in den einfachen Häusern der Küstenregion üblich ist. Der naturbelassene Garten mit Mandelbäumen, Kokospalmen und anderen einheimischen Obstbäumen des Atlantischen Regenwaldes wurde lediglich um Orchideen, Epidendren und Bromelien bereichert, welche die Hausherrin selbst pflanzte.

Egalement connu sous le nom de Praia do Espelho, le hameau de Curuípe est situé au sud de Trancoso, en contrebas de Vila do Outeiro. Par choix de ses habitants et des estivants, on ne trouve pas de grandes villas luxueuses, mais des petites maisons de pêcheur reflétant le charme et le bon goût de leurs propriétaires cosmopolites. Pour ces personnes, qui vivent généralement dans les grandes villes du Brésil, le luxe est de pouvoir se réveiller et de marcher pieds nus dans le sable, de se baigner dans la mer au coucher du soleil. C'est exactement ce que la paysagiste Isabel Duprat recherchait quand elle a décidé d'alterner sa vie professionnelle à São Paulo avec des moments de détente à Praia do Espelho. Elle a conservé l'architecture de la maison où elle passe tout l'été : une seule chambre à coucher, une petite salle à manger à vivre équipée d'un coin cuisine et la salle de bains à l'extérieur de la maison, comme c'est généralement le cas pour les maisons simples de l'intérieur du pays. Au paysage naturel (dans lequel prospèrent amandiers, cocotiers et de nombreuses espèces d'arbres fruitiers du littoral) la maîtresse de maison n'a ajouté que quelques plantes, telles que des orchidées ou des broméliacées.

LEFT:
The hammock, typical of northeast Brazil, is tied to the trunks of the coconut and almond trees to provide a place to rest and enjoy the sea breeze off the tranquil waters.

RIGHT ABOVE:
The dining table is in the area outside the house, under a fabric canopy affording protection against the sun or rain.

RIGHT BELOW:
In the reading corner, the ceramic tabletop with little roses is by the artist João Calazans. The fuxico cushion, handmade from fabric remnants, echoes the design.

LINKE SEITE:
Die Hängematte, eine Handarbeit aus Bahia, ist zwischen einer Kokospalme und einem Mandelbaum gespannt und wird von der frischen Meeresbrise umspielt.

RECHTS OBEN:
Der Esstisch im Freien ist durch ein Segeltuch vor Sonne und Regen geschützt.

RECHTS UNTEN:
Der Beistelltisch mit Rosenmuster wurde von dem Künstler João Calazans gefertigt. Das Kissen im fuxico-Design greift das Tischmuster auf.

PAGE DE GAUCHE :
Le hamac typique du nordest du Brésil, accroché au tronc d'un cocotier et d'un amandier, est l'endroit idéal pour se reposer en profitant de la brise marine.

À DROITE, EN HAUT :
La table de repas, installée à l'extérieur de la maison, est protégée du soleil et de la pluie par un écran de tissu.

À DROITE, EN BAS :
Dans le coin réservé à la lecture, le plateau de table en céramique orné de petites roses est l'œuvre de l'artiste João Calazans. Le coussin au crochet, fait à la main avec des chutes de tissu, reproduit le même motif.

ISABEL DUPRAT & MANUEL LEÃO / CURUÍPE

LEFT PAGE:
There are examples of local handicrafts, such as the coconut wood screen and the flower rug made from fabric scraps, in every corner of the house.

RIGHT PAGE:
The large rustic sofa was made in Trancoso, as was most of the furniture in the house. Once again the fabric features flowers, reflecting the lady of the house's attachment to them.

LINKE SEITE:
Beispiele des lokalen Kunsthandwerks, wie die Jalousie aus Kokosholz oder der Blumenteppich aus Stoffresten, finden sich überall im Haus.

RECHTE SEITE:
Das breite, rustikale Sofa wurde wie die meisten Möbel des Hauses in Trancoso gefertigt. Das Blumenmuster des Bezugs verweist auf die Leidenschaft der Hausherrin.

PAGE DE GAUCHE :
Des objets d'artisanat local, comme le store en bois de cocotier et le tapis à fleurs fabriqué avec des chutes de tissu, sont partout présents.

128

PAGE DE DROITE :
Le grand canapé rustique a été fabriqué à Trancoso, comme la plupart des meubles de la maison. Le tissu qui le recouvre dénote la passion de la maîtresse de maison pour les fleurs.

LEFT PAGE:
The wooden ladder leads to the mezzanine, which serves as a guest room. On the wall, the fish- and turtle-shaped coat hooks are also the work of Calazans.

RIGHT PAGE:
The ceiling in the master bedroom is lined with straw from the dendê tree, which produces a small coconut from which a yellow oil, much used in Bahia cookery, is extracted.

LINKE SEITE:
Die Leiter führt zum Mezzanin, das als „Gästezimmer" dient. Die Wandhaken in Form eines Fisches und einer Schildkröte wurden wieder von João Calazans geschaffen.

RECHTE SEITE:
Die Decke des ehelichen Schlafzimmers ist mit Fasern der Kokospalme dendê verkleidet, aus deren kleinen Kokosnüssen auch das bekannte gelbe Öl gewonnen wird, welches man in der bahianischen Küche verwendet.

PAGE DE GAUCHE :
L'échelle en bois mène à la mezzanine qui sert de chambre d'amis. Au mur, les portemanteaux en forme de poisson et de tortue sont aussi de Calazans.

PAGE DE DROITE :
Le plafond de la chambre à coucher du couple est recouvert de paille tressée de palmier à huile. On extrait de ses petites noix une huile jaune, très utilisée dans la cuisine bahianaise.

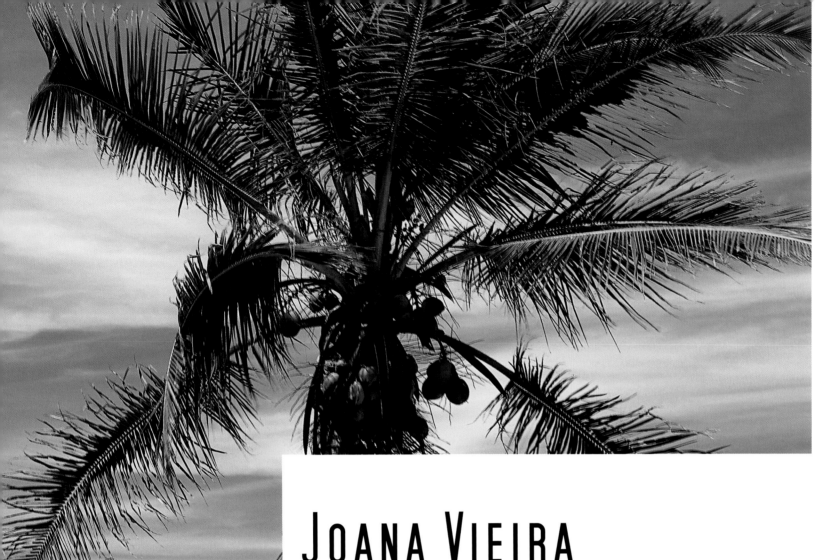

JOANA VIEIRA

CURUÍPE

In 1997, the São Paulo artist and designer Joana Vieira went to Sul da Bahia and has never left. She fell in love with the almost virgin landscape of Espelho das Maravilhas, one of the most beautiful beaches in Sul da Bahia. It is in an area known as the "Costa do Descobrimento" (Discovery Coast), because it was the first region of Brazil encountered by Portuguese explorer Pedro Álvares Cabral in 1500. Six years later, Joana put down her roots, smartened up the little former schoolhouse on Espelho beach and made it her bayside *pied-à-terre*. Surrounded by the blue of the Atlantic Ocean and the green of the native trees, the little house occupies a mere 160 square metres or so and has only one bedroom, a living room, a bathroom and a kitchen. The *redário* (outdoor hammock area) is in the huge coconut grove by the water's edge. With most of the furniture made in Trancoso, the house derives its great charm from the cheerful décor, which is truly Brazilian in character and was created by the lady of the house from a profusion of everyday raw materials which lend it a distinct charm.

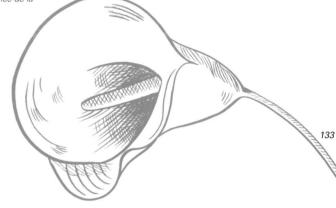

133

Die Künstlerin und Designerin Joana Vieira aus São Paulo kam 1997 in den Süden Bahias – und blieb dort. Die ursprüngliche Schönheit des Strandes Espelho das Maravilhas („Wunderspiegel"), eines der schönsten Strände im Süden Bahias, verzauberte sie. Dies soll der erste Landstrich gewesen sein, der vom Entdecker Brasiliens, dem portugiesischen Seefahrer Pedro Álvares Cabral, im Jahre 1500 gesichtet wurde. Joana Vieira beschloss nach sechs Jahren, hier für immer Wurzeln zu schlagen. Sie renovierte das kleine Haus, das früher eine Schule beherbergt hatte, und richtete sich ihr Pied-à-terre am Strand ein. Vom Blau des Atlantiks und vom Grün der Wälder umgeben, beherbergt das rund 160 Quadratmeter große Haus lediglich ein Schlafzimmer, ein Wohnzimmer, Bad und Küche, ergänzt durch einen *redário*, einen für Hängematten bestimmten Bereich im ausladenden Palmenhain vor dem Haus. Die Inneneinrichtung mit den meist in Trancoso hergestellten Möbeln erhält durch das insgesamt verspielte Dekor einen besonderen Charme. Die mit typisch brasilianischem Feeling zusammengestellte Mischung von groben Materialien und ein wenig Kitsch ist die Handschrift der Hausherrin.

En 1997, l'artiste en arts plastiques et designer Joana Vieira, vivant alors à São Paulo, est arrivée dans cette région située au sud de l'Etat de Bahia pour ne plus la quitter. Elle est tombée sous l'enchantement du paysage quasiment vierge d'Espelho das Maravilhas, l'une des plus belles plages au sud de Bahia, dans une région connue sous le nom de Côte de la Découverte pour avoir été la première terre brésilienne visitée par le navigateur portugais Pedro Álvares Cabral en l'an 1500. Six ans plus tard, Joana a arrangé la petite maison qui servait de poste sur la plage Espelho das Maravilhas et en a fait son pied-à-terre dans l'Etat de Bahia. Entourée par le bleu de l'Atlantique et le vert des arbres, l'habitation d'environ 160 mètres carrés possède seulement une chambre à coucher, un séjour, une salle de bains, une cuisine et une terrasse abritée par l'immense cocoteraie du bord de mer. Avec son mobilier en grande partie fabriqué à Trancoso, le charme principal de la maison provient de la décoration riante très brésilienne. La maîtresse de maison l'a créée elle-même avec une profusion d'éléments issus de la culture populaire, qui génèrent un certain charme kitsch.

LEFT PAGE:
Like a king, Joana's dog, Bigode, enjoys the sunshine comfortably enthroned on cushions made by the lady of the house in her studio in Trancoso.

RIGHT PAGE:
The outdoor lounge area, or redário, one of Joana's favourite spots, is in the coconut grove facing peaceful Espelho das Maravilhas beach, an irresistible invitation to relax.

LINKE SEITE:
Wie ein König sonnt sich der Mischling Bigode („Schnurrbart") auf Kissen, welche die Hausherrin selbst in ihrem Atelier in Trancoso angefertigt hat.

RECHTE SEITE:
Die Hängematten, auf denen Joana Vieira gern entspannt, schwingen im Schatten der Palmen und bieten einen herrlichen Ausblick auf die Strandidylle.

PAGE DE GAUCHE :
Trônant sur les coussins créés par la maîtresse de maison dans son atelier de Trancoso, Bigode le bâtard profite du soleil.

PAGE DE DROITE :
Un des endroits préférés de Joana, la terrasse abritée par les cocotiers sur la plage Espelho das Maravilhas, invite à la relaxation.

134

Bromeliads and orchids, native to the Atlantic Forest, are the mainstay of the garden, which also features lush fruit trees, including mangos, cashews and almonds.

Bromelien und Orchideen, Gewächse des Atlantischen Regenwaldes, schmücken den Garten, dessen üppige Bäume Mangos, Cashewnüsse, Mandeln und andere Früchte tragen.

Le jardin, composé de broméliacées et d'orchidées indigènes du littoral atlantique, est aussi peuplé d'arbres fruitiers exubérants tels que manguiers, amandiers et anacardiers.

136

LEFT ABOVE:
Tiny details contribute charm and cheerfulness to the house, such as the hummingbird water fountain and the curtains tied back with fabric flowers.

LEFT BELOW:
The daisy-shaped lampshade is made of coconut fibre, a regional handicraft.

RIGHT:
The bamboo pergola shelters the image of Yemanjá, the Ocean Queen, a figure born of religious syncretism.

LINKS OBEN:
Kleine Details, wie die verspielten Kolibritränken oder die mit Stoffblumen zusammengehaltenen Vorhänge, verleihen dem Haus Charme und Heiterkeit.

LINKS UNTEN:
Der margeritenförmige Lampenschirm aus Kokosfasern wurde von lokalen Kunsthandwerkern gefertigt.

RECHTE SEITE:
Unter dem Bambusdach der Veranda befindet sich eine Statue der Yemanjá, der „Königin des Meeres".

À GAUCHE, EN HAUT :
De petits détails égaient la maison tels l'abreuvoir destiné aux colibris et les rideaux attachés avec des fleurs en tissu.

À GAUCHE, EN BAS :
Le lustre en forme de marguerite, un objet d'artisanat local, est réalisé en fibre de coco.

PAGE DE DROITE :
La pergola en bambou tressé abrite une statue de Yemanjá, déesse de la mer dans le syncrétisme religieux afro-brésilien.

JOANA VIEIRA / CURUÍPE

LEFT:
*The living room brings
together a number of
elements characteristic
of Brazilian popular culture:
the white lace tablecloth,
images of saints crafted by
Joana and the chitão printed fabric covering the sofa.*

RIGHT ABOVE:
*This simple but attractive
key-ring is made of fabric
scraps.*

RIGHT BELOW:
*The colours of the Brazilian
flag are green to represent
the country's forests, yellow
for its wealth in gold and
blue for the sky.*

LINKE SEITE:
*Im Wohnzimmer treffen
Objekte der brasilianischen
Volkskultur aufeinander:
eine Tischdecke aus weißer
Spitze, von Joana gestalte-
te Heiligenbilder und ein
farbenfroher Sofaüberwurf.*

RECHTS OBEN:
*Der entzückende Schlüs-
selanhänger besteht aus
Stoffresten.*

RECHTS UNTEN:
*Das Grün der brasilianischen
Fahne steht für den Wald-
reichtum des Landes, das
Gelb für seine Schätze und
das Blau für den Himmel.*

PAGE DE GAUCHE :
*La salle à manger
rassemble divers éléments
caractéristiques de la
culture populaire
brésilienne : une nappe
en dentelle blanche, des
statuettes de saints
personnalisées par Joana
et un tissu en coton
imprimé sur le canapé.*

À DROITE, EN HAUT :
*Le curieux porte-clés de
style naïf est fabriqué avec
des chutes de tissu.*

À DROITE, EN BAS :
*Les couleurs du drapeau
brésilien, le vert, le jaune
et le bleu, évoquent les
forêts, la richesse et le ciel
du Brésil.*

JOANA VIEIRA / CURUÍPE

LEFT ABOVE:
The wall has a niche for an image of the Virgin Mary and candleholders, both fashioned crudely in plaster of Paris.

LEFT BELOW:
The image of Yemanjá is hollow and has little holes to reveal the light of the lamp nestled inside.

RIGHT:
Simple and cheerful, the kitchen has its pans, crockery and cutlery on display.

LINKS OBEN:
Die Wandnische für Marienfigur und die Kerzenhalter sind aus Gips gefertigt.

LINKS UNTEN:
Die hohle Yemanjá-Statue hat kleine Löcher durch die das Licht scheinen kann.

RECHTE SEITE:
In der einfachen, freundlichen Küche sind Töpfe, Teller und Besteck immer zur Hand.

À GAUCHE, EN HAUT :
La niche murale pour la Vierge et les porte-bougies sont en plâtre.

À GAUCHE, EN BAS :
La statue de Yemanjá est creuse et comporte de petits orifices par lesquels passe la lumière de la lampe placée à l'intérieur.

PAGE DE DROITE :
Simple et joyeuse, la cuisine laisse les ustensiles à portée de main.

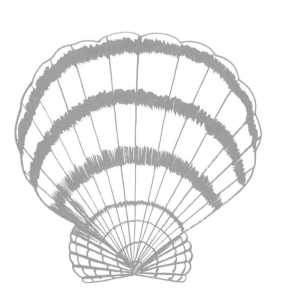

JOANA VIEIRA / CURUÍPE

LEFT PAGE:
The ribbons for Our Lord of Bonfim, originally a religious symbol, which the superstitious tie around their wrists for luck, are put to novel use as a form of decoration.

RIGHT PAGE:
Behind the bed, with its fuxico bedspread – a craft typical of northeast Brazil – is a small altar with images representing various religions.

LINKE SEITE:
Traditionelle Glücksbänder aus Bahia, die eigentlich am Handgelenk getragen werden, wurden zu Dekorationszwecken umfunktioniert.

RECHTE SEITE:
Hinter dem mit einer typisch brasilianischen Tagesdecke geschmückten Bett verbirgt sich ein Altar mit Symbolen verschiedener Religionen.

PAGE DE GAUCHE :
Les rubans dédiés au Senhor do Bonfim. Au départ symbole religieux, ils sont utilisés comme bracelets porte-bonheur et ici comme élément décoratif.

PAGE DE DROITE :
Derrière le lit à couverture artisanale au crochet, typique du nord-est du Brésil, se trouve un petit autel garni de statuettes représentant diverses religions.

Fazenda Calá

JOÃO CALAZANS
BARRA DO PRATEAÇU

The colours of the Brazilian flag are green, yellow and blue, representing the lushness of its forests, its wealth in gold and the clarity of the sky. In the case of the landscape surrounding Fazenda Calá, the banks of the Prateaçu river on Espelho das Maravilhas beach, the colours of the flag shine bright but the green is now that of the sea and the yellow that of the fine sand that tempts visitors and residents to sunbathe. Only the blue still relates to the glorious sky. The artist João Calazans came to this region back in the 1970s. He set up home here, started to produce his sculptures with local clay and began to build the ranch with such materials as he was able to transport there, since access was difficult at the time. For that reason sand, concrete and earthenware bricks were the building blocks for the rounded contours, white walls and blue windows. The house was designed with an almost monastic simplicity by its owner, who would rather live in harmony with nature than amass material possessions.

LEFT PAGE:
The beach, almost deserted throughout the year, sports the occasional rough and ready hut thatched with coconut straw.

RIGHT:
The winds blowing in from the sea are a balm on sunny days.

FOLLOWING DOUBLE PAGE, LEFT AND RIGHT:
The scene is like a water-colour painted in the colours of Brazil. The residents of the ranch enjoy having the beach on their doorstep.

LINKE SEITE:
An dem meistens men-schenleeren Strand stehen hier und da schlichte Kokosnussstrohdächer zum Sonnenschutz.

RECHTS:
Die Winde vom Meer sind eine Wohltat an sonnigen Tagen.

FOLGENDE DOPPELSEITE, LINKS UND RECHTS:
Die brasilianischen Farben in der Landschaft präsentieren sich den Fazenda-Bewoh-nern als ein natürliches Gemälde.

PAGE DE GAUCHE :
Un abri couvert de paille de cocotier sur la plage, prati-quement déserte pendant l'année.

À DROITE :
Le vent marin apporte une fraîcheur appréciée les jours ensoleillés.

DOUBLE PAGE SUIVANTE, À GAUCHE ET À DROITE :
Les couleurs du drapeau brésilien composent l'aqua-relle du paysage qui s'offre à la vue depuis la ferme.

147

Die Farben der brasilianischen Fahne – Grün, Gelb und Blau – re-präsentieren den Waldreichtum und die Goldschätze des Landes sowie die Klarheit des Himmels. In der Landschaft um die Fazen-da Calá, gelegen am Ufer des Flusses Prateaçu und am Strand Espelho das Maravilhas, werden diese Farben lebendig, wenn auch neu interpretiert: Das Grün findet sich im Meer wieder und das Gelb im feinen Sand, der zum Sonnenbaden einlädt. Das Blau bleibt weiterhin dem herrlichen Himmel vorbehalten. Der Künstler João Calazans kam in den 1970er-Jahren hierher. Er ließ sich nie-der und begann, seine Skulpturen aus lokalem Ton zu fertigen. Und er errichtete sein Haus mit solchen Materialien, die er, trotz des schwierigen Zugangs zum Grundstück, bis dorthin transportie-ren konnte. Daher bilden Sand, Beton und Tonziegel die Grundlage des Gebäudes, das sich durch abgerundete Formen, weiße Wände und blaue Fenster auszeichnet. Das Haus, von einer fast asketischen Schlichtheit, wurde vom Hausherrn selbst entworfen, dem es wichtiger ist, naturverbunden zu leben, als materielle Güter um sich zu sammeln.

Les couleurs du drapeau brésilien, le vert, le jaune et le bleu, évoquent l'exubérance des forêts, la richesse de l'or et la clarté du ciel. Dans le cas du paysage qui entoure la Fazenda Calá, au bord du fleuve Prateaçu, sur la plage Espelho das Maravilhas, les cou-leurs du drapeau sont présentes mais dans une version légère-ment différente : le vert représente la mer et le jaune, le sable fin qui invite au bain de soleil. Quant au bleu, il reste celui du ciel, splendide. L'artiste plasticien João Calazans est arrivé dans cette région dans les années 1970. Il s'y est établi et a commencé à pro-duire ses sculptures en argile et à bâtir une ferme avec les maté-riaux qu'il a pu transporter en cet endroit, d'accès difficile à cette époque. Pour cette raison, le sable, le ciment et la brique sont les matériaux de base de cette construction aux contours arrondis, aux murs blancs et aux fenêtres bleues. D'une simplicité quasi monastique, la maison a été dessinée par son propriétaire, qui pré-fère vivre en harmonie avec la nature plutôt que d'accumuler les biens matériels.

LEFT:
Three wooden posts are all that is needed to make the hammock area. The table in the centre is one of Calazans's creations made from local clay, which has a high iron content.

RIGHT ABOVE AND BELOW:
The walls of the staircase have no sharp corners and are reminiscent of ancient structures, such as the old Bahia forts built in the 16th and 17th centuries.

LINKE SEITE:
Drei Holzpfähle genügen, um die Hängematten zu befestigen. Zwischen ihnen steht ein von Calazans gefertigter Tisch aus einheimischem, stark eisenhaltigem Ton.

RECHTS OBEN UND UNTEN:
Die Treppenmauern mit abgerundeten Brüstungen erinnern an die alten Forts, wie sie in Bahia im 17. und 18. Jahrhundert errichtet wurden.

PAGE DE GAUCHE :
Trois poteaux en bois ont suffi pour réaliser l'aire d'accrochage des hamacs. La table au centre est l'une des pièces créées par Calazans avec de l'argile locale, riche en fer.

À DROITE, EN HAUT ET EN BAS :
L'escalier aux angles arrondis rappelle les constructions anciennes telles que les vieux forts de l'Etat de Bahia, érigés au XVIᵉ et au XVIIᵉ siècle.

FAZENDA CALÁ / BARRA DO PRATEAÇU

LEFT PAGE:
Coffee time is exquisite. The hand-painted cotton tablecloth was bought in Trancoso.

RIGHT PAGE:
The burned concrete flooring had grooves scored into it to mimic the appearance of wooden boards. On the wall, the nautilus-shaped sconce is another piece by Calazans.

LINKE SEITE:
Der Kaffee wird auf einer handbemalten Tischdecke aus Trancoso serviert.

RECHTE SEITE:
Der Boden aus poliertem Beton wurde mit an Holzdielen erinnernder Maserung versehen. Die muschelförmige Wandleuchte ist ein weiteres Werk Calazans'.

PAGE DE GAUCHE :
Détails de la vaisselle à l'heure du café, sur une nappe en coton peinte à la main achetée à Trancoso.

PAGE DE DROITE :
Le sol en ciment brûlé a été rainuré pour imiter un plancher. Au mur, l'applique en forme de corne d'abondance est signée Calazans.

154

LEFT ABOVE AND BELOW:
There are hardly any cup-board doors in the house. In the kitchen, cotton curtains take the place of doors. The colouring of the scarf echoes that of the house.

RIGHT:
For practical reasons, Calazans preferred most of the furniture to be masonry, such as the sofa in the living room, which is topped with cotton cushions.

LINKS OBEN UND UNTEN:
Kaum ein Schrank hat hier Türen, in der Küche hängen stattdessen Baumwolltücher davor. Die Farben des Schals enthalten die Farben des Hauses.

RECHTE SEITE:
Aus praktischen Gründen entschied Calazans, haupt-sächlich gemauerte Möbel zu verwenden. Das Sofa im Wohnzimmer wird mit weißen, weichen Baumwollkis-sen ergänzt.

À GAUCHE, EN HAUT
ET EN BAS :
La plupart des armoires n'ont pas de portes. Dans la cuisine, des rideaux remplacent la porte. Les couleurs du foulard s'accordent avec celles de la maison.

PAGE DE DROITE :
Pour des raisons pratiques, Cazalans a préféré que la majorité des meubles soient réalisés en maçonnerie, comme le canapé du living, recouvert de coussins en coton blanc.

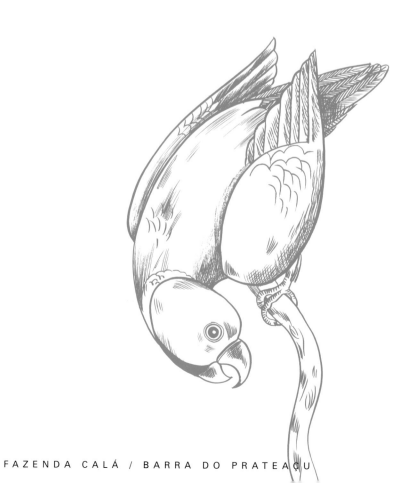

FAZENDA CALÁ / BARRA DO PRATEAÇU

LEFT PAGE:
A pail, the type commonly found in markets in inland Bahia, is used as a shower. Calazans likes to heat water with pitanga leaves for a scented, relaxing bath.

RIGHT PAGE:
The narrow entrance to the toilet is decorated with little sculptures of fish and starfish.

LINKE SEITE:
Ein einfacher Blecheimer wurde in eine Dusche um-gewandelt. Calazans mischt dem Wasser gern Blätter des Baumes pitanga bei, um ein aromatisches und ent-spannendes Duscherlebnis zu erzielen.

RECHTE SEITE:
Der schmale Durchgang zur Toilette wurde mit kleinen Gipsdetails in Form von Fischen und Seesternen versehen.

PAGE DE GAUCHE :
Un seau, d'un type couram-ment rencontré sur les marchés de l'Etat de Bahia, est utilisé pour le système de douche. Cazalans a l'ha-bitude d'ajouter des feuilles de pitanga à l'eau chaude pour prendre un bain parfumé et relaxant.

158

PAGE DE DROITE :
L'entrée étroite des toilettes a été décorée de petites sculptures en forme de poisson et d'étoile de mer.

FAZENDA ESPELHO DA MARAVILHA

ANGELA MASSI, ESPELHO DAS MARAVILHAS

Like the majority of the first newcomers to Trancoso at the end of the 1970s, Angela Massi abandoned the grey of São Paulo in search of sun and sea. All she wanted was to be able to wake up in the morning and dive straight into the blue ocean, and nearly 30 years later she has kept up that daily ritual. What today is Espelho da Maravilha Ranch was no more than a fisherman's cottage on a stretch of sand facing the Atlantic when she bought it. Angela kept the cottage, converted as accommodation for visiting friends, and built her main home on the hill to better enjoy the beautiful view. She often spends long periods at the ranch cultivating coconut, especially during the Brazilian summer, from December to March. The house is filled with objects and furniture that evoke happy memories of her youth, when she would spend her holidays at her grandmother Angelina's coffee plantation in northern Paraná. As Angela often says, it is a piece of paradise, where she is merely the guardian and where she can indulge in her favourite hobby of gardening, planting poincianas and hibiscus (more than a thousand different varieties) and reforesting the area by planting native trees such as *dendê* and *piaçava*.

LEFT PAGE:
The new house was built on the higher part of the grounds, with beautiful views out to sea.

RIGHT:
The main gate to the house is the kind typically used in ranches.

LINKE SEITE:
Das neue Haus wurde im höher gelegenen Grundstücksbereich erbaut, von dem man eine schöne Sicht auf die Küste hat.

RECHTS:
Das Grundstück betritt man durch ein traditionelles Fazenda-Tor.

PAGE DE GAUCHE :
La nouvelle maison a été bâtie sur la partie haute du terrain qui offre une vue magnifique sur la mer.

À DROITE :
Le portail d'entrée à claire-voie est typique des fermes de la région.

Wie die meisten Neuankömmlinge in Trancoso Ende der 1970er-Jahre kam auch Angela Massi aus dem hektischen São Paulo auf der Suche nach Sonne und Meer. Sie wollte morgens aufwachen und direkt in den blauen Ozean springen, und dieses Ritual vollzieht sie bis heute. Ihre Fazenda Espelho da Maravilha war beim Kauf lediglich ein Stück Strand am Atlantik mit einem kleinen Fischerhaus. Angela renovierte das kleine Haus, das heute als Gästezimmer dient, und errichtete das Haupthaus in einer höheren Lage, um die schöne Sicht genießen zu können. Die Fazenda ist eine Kokosplantage, auf der Angela viele Monate, vor allem im brasilianischen Sommer, lebt. Die Einrichtung erinnert die Hausherrin an die Ferien, die sie als Kind auf der Kaffeeplantage ihrer Großmutter Angelina im Bundesstaat Paraná verbrachte. Das Haus sei ein Stück Paradies, das sie lediglich bewache, pflegt sie zu sagen. Sie geht hier ihrem Lieblingshobby – der Gärtnerei – nach, pflanzt Flammenbäume und über tausend Arten von Hibiskus und forstet das Grundstück mit einheimischen Bäumen wie *dendê* oder *piaçava* auf.

Comme la plupart des personnes arrivées à Trancoso à la fin des années 1970, Angela Massi a quitté la grisaille de São Paulo pour trouver le soleil et la mer. Tout ce qu'elle désirait était d'aller se baigner dans l'océan bleu d'azur dès le réveil. La Fazenda Espelho da Maravilha n'était alors qu'une petite maison de pêcheur construite sur le sable, en face de l'océan Atlantique. Angela Massi a conservé la maison, convertie pour pouvoir héberger des amis, et a bâti l'habitation principale sur la partie haute du terrain, pour profiter de la vue. Elle passe souvent de longues périodes dans la ferme à cultiver les noix de coco, en particulier pendant l'été brésilien, entre décembre et mars. Remplie d'objets et de meubles qui lui rappellent ses souvenirs d'enfance, les vacances dans la plantation de café de sa grand-mère Angelina, au nord de l'Etat du Paraná, la maison est, comme sa maîtresse a l'habitude de le dire, « un coin de paradis dont elle est la seule gardienne ». Elle peut s'adonner ici à son passe-temps favori, le jardinage, plantant des flamboyants, des hibiscus (plus de mille variétés différentes) et reboisant la propriété avec des essences indigènes comme le palmier à huile et le palmier piassava.

RIGHT:
Life in the house revolves around the veranda, which links the entertaining spaces to the bedrooms. The furniture was made in Ceará from a type of vine wood.

FOLLOWING DOUBLE PAGE:
A half-wall separates the living room from the kitchen. Both rooms are surrounded by windows on all sides, so that wherever you are the sea and the coconut grove are always in view.

RECHTS:
Die Veranda ist der Dreh- und Angelpunkt des Hauses und verbindet den Wohnbereich mit den Schlafzimmern. Die Möbel aus cipó wurden im Bundesstaat Ceará gefertigt.

FOLGENDE DOPPELSEITE:
Eine kleine Mauer trennt die Küche vom Wohnzimmer, dessen zu allen Seiten gewandte Fenster dem Betrachter immer einen Blick auf das Meer und den Kokoshain ermöglichen.

À DROITE:
La vie se déroule autour de la terrasse, lien entre l'espace de vie sociale et les chambres à coucher. Le mobilier en bois d'une variété de cipo a été fabriqué dans l'Etat du Ceará.

DOUBLE PAGE SUIVANTE :
Une demi-cloison sépare la salle à manger de la cuisine. Cette partie de la maison, entièrement entourée de fenêtres, offre une vue splendide sur la mer et sur la cocoteraie.

162

Nana Salles & Flávio Marelim

CARAÍVA

From Porto Seguro to the extreme south of Bahia, there are a string of coastal villages such as Arraial D'Ajuda, Trancoso, Curuípe, Caraíva, Corumbau and Cumuruxatiba, to mention just the more famous ones. There are special beaches in all of these seaside towns. One of these is the Ponta do Camarão beach in Caraíva, the location chosen by Rio innkeepers Nana Salles and Flávio Marelim for their home on the southern coast of Bahia. The little wooden house, measuring just 75 square metres, is in the heart of a plot of land one thousand times bigger than the area built on, amid lush vegetation with 100-year-old native trees, and just five metres from the beach. The couple, who own the charming hotel that bears the name of the beach, exchanged Rio de Janeiro for the peace of Caraíva to provide a better quality of life for their small children, Bento and Flora, closer to nature and with a simpler lifestyle. This also brought them closer to their guests, whom they pamper with every comfort of modern life, albeit with the warmth and care of a bygone era.

Two parallel coconut palms serve as a gateway to the entrance of the brightly painted house surrounded by greenery.

Ein Portal aus zwei Kokospalmen führt zum Eingang des farbenfrohen und von Pflanzen umgebenen Hauses.

Deux cocotiers parallèles servent de portail d'entrée à la maison aux couleurs vives entourée par la végétation.

Zwischen Porto Seguro und dem äußersten Süden Bahias zeigt die Küstenkarte Dörfer wie Arraial D'Ajuda, Trancoso, Curuípe, Caraíva, Corumbau und Cumuruxatiba, um nur die bekannteren zu nennen. Jeder dieser Küstenorte besitzt besondere, mehr oder weniger stark besuchte Strände. Einer der einsameren Strände ist Ponta do Camarão in Caraíva. Nana Salles und Flávio Marelim, ein Hotelierehepaar aus Rio de Janeiro, erkoren diesen Ort zu ihrem Domizil in Bahia. Das kleine Holzhaus mit lediglich 75 Quadratmetern Wohnfläche steht inmitten eines rund tausendmal größeren Grundstücks, umgeben von einer üppigen Vegetation mit jahrhundertealten einheimischen Bäumen und noch dazu nur fünf Meter vom Strand entfernt. Das Ehepaar hat Rio de Janeiro gegen Caraíva getauscht, vor allem um seine Kinder Bento und Flora unkompliziert und naturverbunden aufwachsen zu sehen. Es besitzt auch ein Hotel in Caraíva, so können die Eheleute gleichzeitig ihren Hotelgästen näher sein, die sie gern mit allen Bequemlichkeiten des modernen Lebens sowie mit der Wärme und Herzlichkeit der alten Zeiten verwöhnen.

De Porto Seguro jusqu'à la pointe sud de l'Etat de Bahia, la carte indique une succession de hameaux tels qu'Arraial D'Ajuda, Trancoso, Curuípe, Caraíva, Corumbau et Cumuruxatiba, pour ne citer que les plus connus. Chacune de ces bourgades du littoral possède des plages au caractère particulier, plus ou moins fréquentées. C'est le cas de Ponta do Camarão, à Caraíva, que le couple d'hôteliers originaires de Rio de Janeiro, Nana Salles et Flávio Marelim, a choisie comme résidence sur le littoral sud de l'Etat de Bahia. La petite maison en bois, dont la surface est d'à peine 75 mètres carrés, est située à cinq mètres de la plage, au cœur d'un terrain mille fois plus vaste, au milieu d'une végétation luxuriante composée d'arbres indigènes centenaires. Propriétaires de l'hôtel de charme qui porte le nom de la plage, le couple a échangé la vie de Rio de Janeiro contre la paix de Caraíva, afin d'offrir à ses jeunes enfants, Bento et Flora, un mode de vie plus simple et plus proche de la nature. En outre, cela leur permet d'être plus proches de leurs hôtes, auxquels ils fournissent tout le confort de la vie moderne avec en plus le plaisir d'un accueil chaleureux à l'ancienne.

LEFT PAGE:
Although the house nestles in the middle of a forest, the couple does not forego the comforts of cosy sofas and a soft carpet made of natural cotton fibre.

RIGHT PAGE:
The family like to sit round the colonial-style table for long chats after meals. The wooden counter serves as a sideboard and below it is a crockery cupboard.

LINKE SEITE:
Auch wenn sie mitten in der Natur wohnen, verzichten die Hausherren nicht auf den Komfort von gemütlichen Sofas und eines weichen Teppichs aus Baumwollfasern.

RECHTE SEITE:
Der Tisch im Kolonialstil wird oft Zeuge langer abendlicher Gesprächsrunden. Die Arbeitsplatte aus Holz dient als Abstellfläche und unten als Geschirrschrank.

PAGE DE GAUCHE :
Bien que la maison soit située au milieu de la forêt, le couple ne dédaigne pas les canapés confortables et la douceur du tapis en coton naturel.

168

PAGE DE DROITE :
Après les repas, la famille aime se rassembler pour discuter autour de la table de style colonial. Sous le plan de travail en bois, une étagère permet de ranger la vaisselle.

LEFT PAGE, RIGHT ABOVE AND BELOW:
The spacious master bedroom is that much cosier thanks to the wooden walls and ceiling. As in nearly every house in the region, a mosquito net is needed over the bed.

FOLLOWING DOUBLE PAGE, LEFT AND RIGHT:
The huge bathroom has no wall to divide it from the outside of the house. The space is completely open and gives onto the forest.

LINKE SEITE SOWIE RECHTS OBEN UND UNTEN:
Die durchgehende Holzverkleidung verleiht dem großzügigen Schlafzimmer des Ehepaares ein angenehmes Wohngefühl. Das Moskitonetz ist in dieser Gegend unverzichtbar.

FOLGENDE DOPPELSEITE, LINKS UND RECHTS:
Keine Wand trennt die großzügige Dusche von der Natur: Der Raum öffnet sich ungehindert zum Wald hin.

PAGE DE GAUCHE, À DROITE EN HAUT ET EN BAS :
Les murs et le plafond en bois réchauffent la vaste chambre à coucher du couple. Le lit est équipé d'une moustiquaire, indispensable dans la région.

DOUBLE PAGE SUIVANTE, À GAUCHE ET À DROITE :
La vaste salle de bains est dénuée de mur sur le côté extérieur, ce qui l'ouvre entièrement sur la forêt.

171

NANA SALLES & FLÁVIO MARELIM / CARAÍVA

FAZENDA BARRA DO CAHY

PRADO

Fazenda Barra do Cahy is south of Corumbau, which in turn is 80 kilometres to the south of the city of Porto Seguro. The main house occupies 500 square metres and was built 170 years ago in hand-worked hardwood. For many years it served as a commercial warehouse, supplying the region with products such as food, kerosene and textiles. The income of the ranch, known as Barra do Cahy or Barra de Santo Antônio (St Anthony being the patron saint of the region), came from exports of wood from the Atlantic Forest. After it was turned into a residence, the old chapel became the best room in the house, with dazzling views of the sea and the Cahy river. All that singular and secular richness has been preserved in the last 30 years by the current owner, an aviator and adventurer who in the 1970s came across the ranch by chance on one of his flights over the Porto Seguro region. Its two kilometres of beach, and the convergence of the sea with the Cahy river (Cahy is an indigenous word meaning "forest river"), set the tone, offering a private view for those who want to see nothing but nature.

Die Fazenda Barra do Cahy liegt unterhalb von Corumbau, das sich wiederum 80 Kilometer südlich von Porto Seguro befindet. Das 500 Quadratmeter große Haupthaus wurde vor rund 170 Jahren gänzlich aus Hartholz gebaut. Jahrelang diente es als Lagerhaus der Region für Lebensmittel, Kerosin, Textilien und andere Produkte. Die Fazenda, auch als „Barra do Cahy" oder „Barra de Santo Antônio" (der Schutzheilige der Region) bekannt, lebte von der Holzgewinnung aus dem Atlantischen Regenwald. Nach ihrer Umwandlung in ein Wohnhaus wurde die ehemalige Kapelle zum besten Zimmer des Hauses, mit atemberaubendem Ausblick auf das Meer und den Fluss Cahy. Um den historischen Bau kümmert sich seit 30 Jahren der jetzige Besitzer, ein Pilot und Abenteurer, der die Fazenda in den 1970er-Jahren zufällig bei einem Flug über der Umgebung von Porto Seguro entdeckte. Der kilometerlange Strand und die Mündung des Flusses Cahy – der indianische Name bedeutet „Fluss aus dem Wald" – beherrschen die herrliche Aussicht vom Haus aus, die dem Betrachter nichts als Natur bietet.

La Fazenda Barra do Cahy se trouve au sud du hameau de Corumbau, lui-même situé à 80 kilomètres au sud de la ville de Porto Seguro. Le bâtiment de 500 mètres carrés a été entièrement construit en bois de charpente, il y a 170 ans. Pendant de nombreuses années, il a été utilisé comme entrepôt commercial pour approvisionner la région en produits divers, notamment en aliments, kérosène et tissus. La ferme, connue sous le nom de Barra do Cahy ou Barra de Santo Antônio, le saint patron local, vivait de l'exploitation du bois de la forêt du littoral pour l'exportation. Après sa transformation en résidence, l'ancienne chapelle est devenue la meilleure chambre de la maison, avec une vue éblouissante sur la mer et sur le fleuve Cahy. Cette richesse à la fois unique et séculaire a été préservée depuis 30 ans par son propriétaire actuel, aviateur et aventurier, qui a découvert la ferme par hasard lors d'un vol au-dessus de la région de Porto Seguro. Lui qui ne souhaite rien voir d'autre que la nature est comblé par le caractère unique des deux kilomètres de plage et de l'embouchure du fleuve Cahy (mot indigène signifiant « fleuve de la forêt »).

PREVIOUS DOUBLE PAGE:
The veranda commands a view of the magnificent greens and blues of the coconut palms, river and sea.

LEFT:
On the front veranda under twin windows is a bench hand-carved from a tree trunk.

RIGHT ABOVE AND BELOW:
The house is totally surrounded by verandas with original wooden flooring. The only change made to the floor is the blue colouring on alternate floorboards.

VORIGE DOPPELSEITE:
Von der Terrasse kann man die grün-blaue Farbexplosion von Kokospalmen, Fluss und Meer genießen.

LINKE SEITE:
Unter den zwei Fenstern der vorderen Veranda steht eine aus einem Baumstamm gefertigte Bank.

RECHTS OBEN UND UNTEN:
Das Haus ist rundum von Veranden mit dem originalen Dielenboden umgeben. Die einzige Veränderung des Bodens sind die im Wechsel blau gestrichenen Bretter.

DOUBLE PAGE PRÉCÉDENTE :
La terrasse permet d'apprécier l'explosion de couleurs vertes et bleues offertes par la cocoteraie, le fleuve et l'océan.

PAGE DE GAUCHE :
Sur la terrasse avant, sous les deux fenêtres, un banc fabriqué artisanalement dans un tronc d'arbre.

À DROITE, EN HAUT ET EN BAS :
La maison est entourée de terrasses dont le plancher est d'origine. La seule intervention a été l'application d'une patine de couleur bleue, en alternance.

179

FAZENDA BARRA DO CAHY / PRADO

LEFT ABOVE AND BELOW:
Period furniture, such as the oval mirror, acts as a counterpoint to the rustic bed with its old wrought-iron bedstead and cotton curtains, evoking a 19th-century atmosphere.

RIGHT:
In the living room with its simple furniture, signal buoys, remnants of sea-going vessels, oars and other items connected with the sea have become part of the décor.

LINKS OBEN UND UNTEN:
Antike Möbel, wie der ovale Spiegel, kontrastieren mit dem rustikalen Bett. Das schmiedeeiserne Bettgitter und die Baumwollvorhänge lassen das 19. Jahrhundert lebendig werden.

RECHTE SEITE:
Im schlicht eingerichteten Wohnzimmer wurden verschiedene nautische Elemente – wie Signalbojen, Schiffsteile, Ruder und Ähnliches – in die Dekoration integriert.

À GAUCHE, EN HAUT ET EN BAS :
Le miroir ovale d'époque fait contrepoint avec le lit rustique à baldaquin et les rideaux en coton, qui recréent l'atmosphère du XIXᵉ siècle.

PAGE DE DROITE :
Dans la salle à manger au mobilier rustique, des bouées de signalisation, des vestiges d'embarcations, des rames et d'autres objets restituent l'ambiance marine.

FAZENDA BARRA DO CAHY / PRADO

Casa de Coral

VERONICA & JAMIE STEWART-GRANGER

CUMURUXATIBA

In 1974, Scottish photographer Jamie Stewart-Granger docked in Brazil. (The familiar surname comes from his famous father, English actor Jimmy Stewart-Granger.) Before going to Sul da Bahia he spent long periods in Rio de Janeiro, São Paulo (where he met his wife, Veronica, a Hungarian artist naturalised as a Brazilian) and Tiradentes, a historic town in Minas Gerais. But his heart beat faster when he discovered Cumuruxatiba, a little paradise 100 kilometres to the south of Trancoso. The climate, which he regards as the best in Brazil, the landscape, which is forever changing on account of the tides and winds, and the house, the oldest in the region, totally covered in coral swept onto the beach by the sea, were all decisive factors in the couple's decision to move to this fishing village. Small and cosy, Casa de Coral is in a small fishing village next to the Descobrimento National Park, created to preserve the fauna and flora in the region where Brazil was first discovered by Europeans in 1500.

LEFT PAGE:
The beach is protected by a coral reef, which keeps the waters calm, although at full moon the tide can be very high.

LEFT:
The Atlantic Forest behind and 100 metres of beach in front of the house preserve this little paradise.

LINKE SEITE:
Ein Korallenriff schützt den Strand gegen die Gezeiten und verhindert die Wellenbildung, wenngleich die Flut bei Vollmond sehr hoch sein kann.

LINKS:
Der Atlantische Regenwald im Hintergrund und ein 100 Meter breiter Strand direkt vor dem Haus verwandeln das Anwesen in ein kleines Paradies.

PAGE DE GAUCHE :
La plage est protégée des vagues par une barrière de corail. La marée monte toutefois de manière impressionnante pendant les périodes de pleine lune.

À GAUCHE :
Avec la forêt atlantique au fond et la plage à 100 mètres devant la maison, cet endroit est un véritable coin de paradis.

Der schottische Fotograf Jamie Stewart-Granger – den Nachnamen erbte er von seinem berühmten Vater, dem Schauspieler Jimmy Stewart-Granger – kam 1974 nach Brasilien. Den Süden Bahias erkundete er erst nach längeren Aufenthalten in Rio de Janeiro, São Paulo – wo er seine Frau Veronica, eine in Brasilien lebende ungarische Künstlerin, kennenlernte – und Tiradentes, einer alten Kolonialstadt in Minas Gerais. Doch sein Herz schlug erst höher, als er Cumuruxatiba entdeckte, ein kleines Paradies südlich von Trancoso. Bei der Entscheidung des Ehepaares, sich in dem Fischerdorf niederzulassen, spielten verschiedene Faktoren mit: das ihrer Meinung nach beste Klima Brasiliens, die unter dem Einfluss des Meeres und der Winde ständig im Wandel befindliche Landschaft und schließlich das Haus, das das älteste der Region ist – bedeckt mit Korallen, die das Meer einst an den Strand spülte. Das kleine, gemütliche „Korallenhaus", wie die Casa de Coral übersetzt heißt, grenzt an den Descobrimento-Nationalpark, wo die Fauna und Flora der Region so erhalten werden soll, wie man sie bei der Entdeckung Brasiliens im Jahre 1500 vorfand.

C'est en 1974 que le photographe écossais Jamie Stewart-Granger (fils de l'acteur anglais Jimmy Stewart-Granger) est arrivé au Brésil. Toutefois, avant de s'installer dans le sud de l'Etat de Bahia, il a d'abord passé de longues périodes à Rio de Janeiro, São Paulo (où il a rencontré son épouse, Veronica, artiste plasticienne hongroise, naturalisée Brésilienne) et Tiradentes, une ville historique du Minas Gerais. Son cœur s'est mis à battre plus fort lorsqu'il a découvert Cumuruxatiba, un coin de paradis à 100 kilomètres au sud de Trancoso. Le climat – le meilleur du Brésil selon lui –, le paysage qui change avec les marées et les vents, et la maison, la plus vieille de la région, entièrement recouverte de corail apporté sur la plage par la mer, ont été les facteurs déterminants dans la décision du couple de venir vivre dans ce hameau de pêcheurs. Petite et accueillante, la Casa de Coral se trouve à côté du parc national Descobrimento, dont l'objectif est de préserver la faune et la flore de la région où le Brésil a été découvert par les Portugais en 1500.

LEFT:
The house acquired a veranda from which you can watch the humpback whales in search of warmer waters in August.

RIGHT ABOVE AND BELOW:
The coral façade, which was the decisive factor in winning over Veronica and Jamie, was entirely hand-crafted by local artisans.

LINKE SEITE:
Von der neu hinzugebauten Veranda des Hauses kann man Buckelwale beob-achten, die im August in die warmen Gewässer kommen.

RECHTS OBEN UND UNTEN:
Die Korallenfassade, die für die Kaufentscheidung von Veronica und Jamie aus-schlaggebend war, wurde von lokalen Handwerkern gefertigt.

PAGE DE GAUCHE :
La maison a été complétée d'une terrasse qui permet d'observer l'arrivée des baleines à bosse au mois d'août, lorsqu'elles recher-chent des eaux plus chaudes.

À DROITE, EN HAUT
ET EN BAS :
La façade en corail, qui a définitivement conquis Veronica et Jamie, a été réalisée par des ouvriers locaux à l'aide d'une technique artisanale.

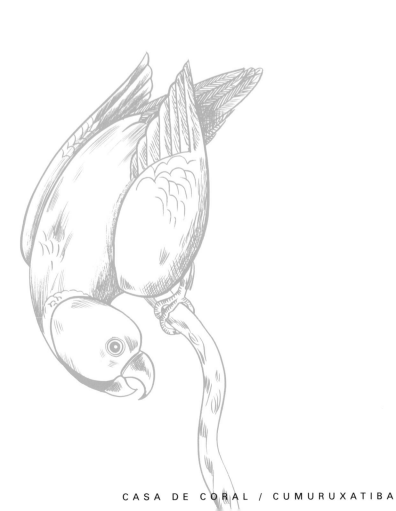

CASA DE CORAL / CUMURUXATIBA

LEFT ABOVE:
The rough wooden stair-case leads to Veronica's studio, on the upper floor, where she paints and weaves using a hand loom.

LEFT BELOW:
The bedroom is a single space with dividing walls, which are also used as bed-steads. The bedspreads made with strips of fabric were bought in Trancoso.

RIGHT:
In the studio, Veronica keeps a collection of teddy bears, which she started when still a child. Next to the door, the item of furniture made from a tree trunk was found in the house and reused as a bar.

LINKS OBEN:
Die rustikale Holztreppe führt zu Veronicas Atelier im Obergeschoss, wo sie malt und webt.

LINKS UNTEN:
Das Schlafzimmer ist durch Trennwände unterteilt, die als Bettabschlüsse dienen. Die Bettüberwürfe aus Stoffstreifen wurden in Trancoso gekauft.

RECHTE SEITE:
Im Atelier sitzen Veronicas Teddys, die sie seit ihrer Kindheit sammelt. Das Möbelstück aus einem Baumstamm an der Tür hat das Ehepaar beim Hauskauf vorgefunden und zur Bar umfunktioniert.

À GAUCHE, EN HAUT :
L'escalier en bois brut mène à l'atelier de Veronica, où elle peint et tisse sur un métier manuel.

À GAUCHE, EN BAS :
La chambre à coucher est un espace ouvert, avec des demi-cloisons qui servent en même temps de tête de lit. Les dessus-de-lit, fabriqués avec des bandes de tissu, ont été achetés à Trancoso.

PAGE DE DROITE :
Dans son atelier, Veronica conserve la collection d'ours en peluche commencée dans son enfance. Près de la porte, le meuble réalisé dans un tronc d'arbre et trouvé dans la maison a été converti en bar.

CASA DE CORAL / CUMURUXATIBA

Sítio Natura

FRANS KRAJCBERG

NOVA VIÇOSA

Frans Krajcberg, painter, sculptor, engraver and photographer, is one of Brazil's champions of ecological art. He took his environmental convictions to extremes, building his house on a treetop like a latter-day Robinson Crusoe. Krajcberg has lived in southern Bahia since 1972, after being invited there by his friend Zanine Caldas, an architect who helped him build the house, seven metres above ground level, on the trunk of a 2.6-metre-wide *pequi* tree. The *pequi* is typical of the Brazilian savannah that is also found in southern Bahia. The house, which has a living room, bedroom, bathroom and veranda, is located in Sítio Natura, an area measuring around 1.2 square-kilometres, which still includes part of the Atlantic Forest. The artist has planted more than 10,000 cuttings of native species there. Krajcberg produced a monumental work of art that included sculptures made of dead tree trunks and charred wood. His art is a reflection of the Brazilian landscape, particularly the Amazon Forest, but it also draws attention to his concern for environmental conservation.

Frans Krajcberg, Maler, Bildhauer, Graveur und Fotograf, ist einer der herausragenden Vertreter ökologischer Kunst in Brasilien. Der engagierte Umweltschützer baute wie ein moderner Robinson Crusoe sein Haus auf einem Baum. Krajcberg lebt seit 1972 im Süden Bahias und bat seinen Freund und Architekten Zanine Caldas, das Haus zu entwerfen und zu errichten. Es wurde sieben Meter über dem Boden auf dem 2,60 Meter dicken Stamm eines *pequi*-Baumes gebaut, ein für Brasiliens Landesinnere typischer, aber auch in Bahia üblicher Baum. Das Haus mit einem Wohnzimmer, einem Schlafzimmer, Bad und Terrasse steht auf dem Sítio Natura („Landgut Natur"), einem 1,2 Quadratkilometer großen Grundstück, das zum Teil zum Atlantischen Regenwald gehört. Der Künstler hat dort 10.000 einheimische Bäume gepflanzt. Das umfassende künstlerische Werk Krajcbergs beinhaltet unter anderem Skulpturen aus abgestorbenen und verkohlten Baumstämmen, und spiegelt damit auch sein Engagement für die Natur Brasiliens wider – vor allem den Regenwald am Amazonas – und deren Erhaltung.

L'un des acteurs de l'art écologique au Brésil, Frans Krajcberg (peintre, sculpteur, graveur et photographe) est allé très loin dans son engagement pour la défense de l'environnement, construisant, tel un Robinson Crusoé moderne, sa maison en haut d'un arbre. Vivant au sud de l'Etat de Bahia depuis 1972, il a découvert cette région après y avoir été invité par son ami Zanine Caldas, l'architecte qui l'a aidé à construire sa maison à sept mètres du sol, sur un tronc de *pequi* (arbre caractéristique du Cerrado brésilien, un type de savane arborée, mais également présent au sud de l'Etat de Bahia) de 2,60 mètres de diamètre. La maison, qui comprend un séjour, une chambre, une salle de bains et une terrasse, est située dans le Sítio Natura, une zone de 1,2 kilomètres carrés dans laquelle subsiste un reste de forêt atlantique. L'artiste a planté ici plus de dix mille pieds d'espèces végétales indigènes. Frans Krajcberg a réalisé une œuvre de grande dimension, composée de sculptures réalisées dans des troncs d'arbres morts et de bois calciné. Son travail reflète le paysage brésilien, plus particulièrement la forêt amazonienne, et attire l'attention sur son souci de sauvegarder l'environnement.

LEFT:
The landscape around the building features fruit trees and bushes.

RIGHT ABOVE:
As far as possible, the house was built using reforested wood. Nature is drawn indoors through the large window panes.

RIGHT BELOW:
The house is entered via the all-wood spiral staircase.

FOLLOWING DOUBLE PAGE:
In a corner of the veranda surrounding the house there are several whale bones displayed like sculptures.

LINKE SEITE:
Obstbäume und Büsche bilden das Szenario rund um die Hauskonstruktion.

RECHTS OBEN:
Für das Bauprojekt wurde so weit wie möglich Holz aus Aufforstungen benutzt. Die Natur dringt durch die großen Glasfenster in das Hausinnere.

RECHTS UNTEN:
Über die hölzerne Wendeltreppe gelangt man ins Haus.

FOLGENDE DOPPELSEITE:
Walknochen wurden zu Skulpturen in einer Ecke der Veranda, die das Haus umgibt.

PAGE DE GAUCHE :
Les arbres fruitiers et les arbustes composent le paysage entourant la construction.

À DROITE, EN HAUT :
L'utilisation de bois de reforestation a été privilégiée dans la construction. Les baies vitrées laissent entrer la nature.

À DROITE, EN BAS :
On accède à la maison par un escalier hélicoïdal en bois.

DOUBLE PAGE SUIVANTE :
Dans un angle de la terrasse qui entoure l'habitation, des os de baleine ont acquis le statut d'œuvre d'art.

SÍTIO NATURA / NOVA VIÇOSA

LEFT ABOVE AND RIGHT:
The trunk of the pequi tree supporting the house runs through this quiet corner decorated with small wooden sculptures of banana palms. The chair in the middle bears the artist's signature.

LEFT BELOW:
In the bedroom, the "swan's beak" bed is made of jacarandá, a typical Brazilian hardwood, now extinct.

LINKS OBEN UND RECHTE SEITE:
Der haustragende pequi-Stamm verläuft durch die mit hölzernen Bananenskulpturen geschmückte Ecke. Auch der Stuhl in der Mitte ist eine Arbeit des Künstlers.

LINKS UNTEN:
Das Bett mit „Schwanenkopf"-Verzierungen ist aus dem Edelholz des vom Aussterben bedrohten brasilianischen Jacarandabaums gefertigt.

À GAUCHE, EN HAUT, ET PAGE DE DROITE :
Le tronc de pequi qui soutient la maison traverse un espace décoré de petites sculptures en bois représentant des bananiers. La chaise au milieu porte la griffe de l'artiste.

À GAUCHE, EN BAS :
Dans la chambre, le lit en « bec de cygne » est en jacaranda, un bois noble typiquement brésilien, en voie d'extinction.

SÍTIO NATURA / NOVA VIÇOSA

Addresses / Adressen / Adresses

ARQUITETOS (ARCHITECTS)

BEATRIZ RÉGIS BITTENCOURT
Rua Alameda dos Colibris, s/n
Porto Seguro – BA – CEP 45818-000
Brazil
PHONE: +55 73 36 68 11 54
EMAIL: brb@brbarquitetura.com.br
www.brb.arquitetura.com.br

DAVID BASTOS
Praça dos Tupinambás, 02 – Marina Contorno
Salvador – BA – CEP 400015-161
Brazil
PHONE: +55 71 33 19 53 55
EMAIL: arquitetura@davidbastos.com
www.davidbastos.com

FABRIZIO CECCARELLI
Rua São Clemente, 413 – Botafogo
Rio de Janeiro – RJ – CEP 22260-001
Brazil
PHONE: +55 21 22 86 52 55
FAX: +55 21 22 86 62 31
EMAIL: arquitetura@a3asseroria.com

MARCELO SUZUKI
Rua Patapio Silva, 103 – Jardim das Bandeiras
São Paulo – SP – CEP 05436-010
Brazil
PHONE: +55 11 30 32 07 03
EMAIL: marcelosuzuki.arq@superig.com.br

PAULO JACOBSEN
STUDIO: BERNARDES JACOBSEN
Rua Corcovado, 250 – Jardim Botânico
Rio de Janeiro – RJ – CEP 22460-050
Brazil
FAX: +55 21 25 12 77 43
EMAIL: bjrj@bja.com.br

Alameda Gabriel Monteiro da Silva
1310/61 – Jardim Paulistano
São Paulo – SP – CEP 01442-000
Brazil
FAX: +55 11 30 82 68 34
EMAIL: bjsp@bja.com.br
www.bjaweb.com.br

RICARDO SALEM
Praça São João s/n
Caixa Postal MCPC 20
Porto Seguro – BA – CEP 45818-000
PHONE: +55 73 36 68 11 78
EMAIL: rs.salem@uol.com.br

RUI CÓRES
Praça José Marcelino, 14 Ed.
Cidade de Ilhéus sls. 1013/1014 – Centro
Ilhéus – BA – CEP 45653-030
Brazil
PHONE: +55 73 32 31 13 70/36 34/13 00
EMAIL: ruicores@uol.com.br

SIG BERGAMIN
Rua Cônego Eugênio Leite, 163 – Jardim América
São Paulo – SP – CEP 05415-010
Brazil
PHONE: +55 11 30 81 34 33
FAX: +55 71 30 64 34 90

21, Rue Visconti 2ième étage
75006 Paris
France
PHONE: +33 1 43 25 16 70
EMAIL: sigbergamin@sigbergamin.com.br
www.sigbergamin.com.br

GALERIA (ART GALLERY)

GALERIA PAULO DARZÉ
Rua Dr. Chrysippo de Aguiar 8 – Corredor da Vitória
Salvador – BA – CEP 40081-310
Brazil
PHONE: +55 71 32 67 09 30
EMAIL: paulodarze@terra.com.br
www.paulodarzegaleria.com.br

ARTISTA (ARTIST)

FRANCO CIRRI
Estrada Arraial D'Ajuda
Porto Seguro – BA – CEP 45818-000
Brazil
PHONE: +55 73 36 68 11 02
EMAIL: f.cri@uolo.com.br

PAISAGISTA (LANDSCAPE DESIGNER)

ISABEL DUPRAT PAISAGISMO
R. Ministro Rocha de Azevedo, 456/5º andar
São Paulo – SP – CEP 01410-000
Brazil
PHONE: +55 11 30 88 18 26
EMAIL: isabelduprat@uol.com.br

HOTEL

PONTA DO CAMARÃO
Praia da Ponta do Camarão, s/n
Espelho/Caraíva – BA – CEP 45816-000
Brazil
PHONE: + 55 73 99 79 62 69
EMAIL: flanana@uol.com.br

LOJAS (SHOPS)

MERCADO MODELO
(Brazilian handcrafts)
Praça Cayru – Comércio
Salvador – BA – CEP 40015-900
Brazil
PHONE: +55 71 32 41 28 93

JACARÉ DO BRASIL
(Furniture)
Rua Dr. Mello Alves, 555
São Paulo – SP – CEP 0147-010
Brazil
PHONE: +55 11 30 81 61 09

Praça São João, 13
Trancoso – BA
Brazil
PHONE: +55 73 36 68 14 90

Josep Bertrand, 3
08021 Barcelona
Spain

JOANA VIEIRA ATELIER
(Customized souvenirs from Trancoso)
Praça São João, 172 – Quadrado de Trancoso
Porto Seguro – BA – CEP 458\3-000
Brazil
PHONE: +55 73 36 68 11 10
EMAIL: joanavieira@uol.com.br

CERÂMICA CALAZANS
(Artistic Ceramics & Earthenware)
Praça São João, 19 – Quadrado de Trancoso
Porto Seguro – BA – CEP 45810-000
Brazil
PHONE: +55 73 36 68 11 12
EMAIL: fazendacala@fazendacala.com.br

To stay informed about upcoming TASCHEN
titles, please request our magazine at
www.taschen.com/magazine or write to TASCHEN,
Hohenzollernring 53, D–50672 Cologne, Germany,
contact@taschen.com, Fax: +49-221-254919. We
will be happy to send you a copy of our magazine
which is filled with information about all of our books.

© 2008 TASCHEN GmbH
Hohenzollernring 53, D–50672 Köln
www.taschen.com

Concept, edited and layout by
Angelika Taschen, Berlin
General project management by
Stephanie Bischoff, Cologne
Designed by dieSachbearbeiter.*innen*, Berlin
Illustrations by Olaf Hajek, www.olafhajek.com
Illustrated map by Tanja da Silva, Cologne
English translation by Dennis Wright for
LocTeam, Barcelona
German translation by Magdalena Nowinska for
LocTeam, Barcelona
French translation by Pascal Durand for
LocTeam, Barcelona
Lithography by Thomas Grell, Cologne

Printed in Germany

ISBN 978-3-8365-0478-2
(Edition with English / German cover)
ISBN 978-3-8365-0480-5
(Edition with French cover)

TASCHEN'S LIFESTYLE SERIES
EDITED BY ANGELIKA TASCHEN

"A collection of idyllic villas guaranteed
to make you dream." *–Elle Décoration*, Paris on *Living in Bali*

"An inspiring book to escape into."
–Scottish Sunday Mail, Glasgow on *Living in Bali*

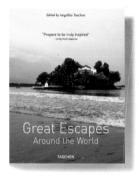

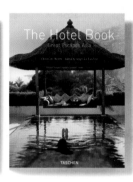

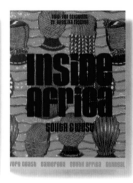
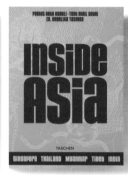

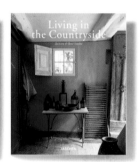

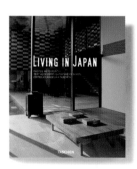

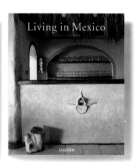
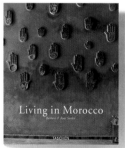
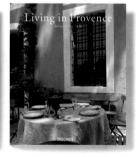

IN PREPARATION

GREAT ESCAPES GERMANY
LIVING IN ARGENTINA
NEW SEASIDE INTERIORS
NEW PARIS INTERIORS
NEW NEW YORK INTERIORS
TASCHEN'S PARIS